Explaining the New America in Plain English

Recent American History for Ordinary People

By Bill Pirkle

Explaining the New America in Plain English.
Copyright © 2010. All rights reserved. Printed in the
United States. No part of this book may be used or
reproduced without the permission of the author.

ISBN 978-0-578-05639-5

This book is dedicated to those Americans who are not happy with the direction that America is headed and to the Founding Fathers who saw this coming and tried to protect us from it.

4

Contents

	Prologue	9
	Forward	11
1	The Two Americas	17
2	Conservatism vs. Liberalism	23
3	The Body Politic	33
4	Lawyers and the Court System	53
5	Our Education System	61
6	The 5th Estate	81
7	The Boomer Effect	85
8	Colleges, the Road to Wealth and Thus Happiness	95
9	Jobs Above All Else	103
10	The New American Culture	117
11	The New Plantation	127
12	The Women's Movement	143

13 Class Warfare	147
14 The Wimpification of America.	155
15 The Softening Military	161
16 Why Racism is Alive and Well and the Race Card	171
17 Foreign Policy	181
18 The United Nations	187
19 The Healthcare System	191
20 Raising Children Today	197
21 Religion in America	207
22 The Great Religious War	215
23 America's Energy Policy and Global Warming	223
24 The Stock Market	233
25 The Minimum Wage	243
26 The Line Item Veto	247
27 The National Debt	253
28 Illegal Immigration	261

Epilogue 265

Prologue

When all is said and done, a case can be made that Americans are not very good citizens. Many don't even vote and few keep up with current events. How many can tell you the name of their congressional representative? How many can tell you how many members there are in the House of Representatives? How many know the size of the national debt? How many could name 5 of the departments of the federal government?

But they are not totally to blame. They have been offered an alternative to good citizenship - entertainment. Regardless of how we stack up to the rest of the world in other areas, there is one area that we excel at - entertainment. We have year round ball games complete with playoffs. We have movies, TV, popular music and more to keep us entertained.

Although most cannot answer the questions above, most could pass a test on movie stars, music stars and sports stars. We have failed to take the advice of some great men -

"The only thing necessary for the triumph of evil is for good men to do nothing." - Edmund Burke

The price of freedom is eternal vigilance -Thomas Jefferson.

We are lacking in both the involvement of good men and vigilance.

But the question is "when you are out to dominate an entire people, how much do you want them to know about government and current affairs and how involved and vigilant do you want them to be?" The best situation is that they sit in front of the TV all day and watch ball games or sitcoms. As long as they are having fun, everything is fine. This allows the status quo to change things slowly and in the background while the public is looking the other way.

It's like the magician who is doing the trick with his left hand while he is showing you his right hand. It's called misdirection.

This book is about the consequences of misdirection.

Forward

For about 60 years American has been at a party. And there is a giant hangover out there with America's name on it.

This is a book about America, how it is and how it was. I decided to write this book because at 67, I am one of a dying breed who remembers first hand how things used to be in America. When my generation is gone in about 15 years there will nobody left who remembers the way we were. Nobody will have lived it. After we are gone, future writers will use video clips, books and news clippings as background for their writings. Given the leftist leanings of the press these days, there is no telling what the future history books will say. Since the winners write the history, these books will no doubt justify everything that has happened as George Orwell predicted.

I recall taking an American history course in college. The professor was constantly reading newspaper articles from the American Revolution, including letters to the editor. It was very enlightening to see what the average American thought about it. One got an entirely different view than what was learned by reading a book on the American Revolution. It was history with a personal touch.

The Ken Burns series on the Civil War was another splendid example because he used so many letters from soldiers and the families of soldiers.

But nobody writes letters these days so that dimension of our understanding will be lost to future historians. Nor do we have bards who hand down stories from one generation to another. It's all on video tape. The movies will be of little use since Hollywood has no problem in altering the facts for the sake of better entertainment.

Here is my first hand knowledge of what happened written by a common man for the common man.

So this book was written for the common man and not for talking heads on TV and others of that ilk. They are invited to read this book, of course, but this book was written in a way that people without a detailed understanding of the American society, politics and economics can understand it. For credibility, I ask the reader to just look around and ask, "is this what I see going on?" Is this, in fact, what has happened?

The chapters are purposely kept short and what is called "supporting detail" as in statistics, charts and graphs are omitted. This is for two reasons. First, all this statistical data is debatable. For every study producing statistics, there is another study reporting different statistics for the same phenomenon. Secondly, there is nothing more boring than reading a lot of charts and graphs. I strived, not for a thick book full of data, but a thin book full of assertions and reasons for why things are the way they are

So I ask the reader to simply take an assertion and ask "is this what I see going on around me? Is this my experience? Do these assertions make sense? Do these explanations make sense? Then vote in 2010 and 2012.

Social problems always go away whether they are solved or not. Why? Because a problem is something that can be compared to a time when this was not a problem. As the people who can remember this time die off, then to those left, this is how it's always been. That is to say this is normal. Take the homeless problem. I think that it is a problem because I can remember a time when there were no homeless people except for people on skid row. For most today, there has always been homeless people roaming the streets begging for money. To the public this is normal and thus this is not a problem, it's normality. So what I would call the homeless problem will just go away as a problem. This is true of all America's so-called problems. Drug use – normal. AIDS deaths – normal, teenage pregnancy – normal, poor performance in school - normal. I think you get the point.

So I decided to write this book to discuss how things are, how things were and why things changed. I have tried to be as objective as I possibly can but many, especially on the Left, will not see this as an objective book. This is true for several reasons. First, many don't see what has happened in this country in the last 50 years, generally under their leadership, as producing any problems at all. They will see this as progress, an increase in the number of freedoms we have. The opposite of "freedom" is "discipline". Secondly, many will think that merely voicing these concerns is a attack on them and the work they have spent their life doing. Finally, many simply think that this is history unfolding and is a normal process.

I can agree somewhat with that last point in that the fall of the Roman Empire was merely history unfolding. That is a dangerous position to take as it excuses every problem as merely history unfolding. That is certainly the easy way out.

But most reasonable people will agree that America has problems today that did not exist for most of our history. My question is what are those problems and why did they occur? What were the forces at play that caused us to have a 50% high school drop out rate in California whose schools were once the envy of the world? Why do we have this humongous national debt and why are we running trade deficits with nearly everyone we trade with?

These are the things I want to explore in this book. I want to compare these times with other times and ask why. I will try to show the causes as I see them.

This book is not a lot of statistics but merely a common sense discussion about our recent history. Each chapter is a summary of the issue and entire books could and have been written on the subject matter in each chapter

There are 28 chapters on many aspects of the American society. Each chapter often explains how it used to be, how it is now and what laws, court interpretations and what underlying social movements caused these changes to produce what many today would say are problems.

So this is really a history book written by, of all people, me, who has a college degree in Mathematics. So what qualifies someone with a degree in Mathematics to write a history book? Well first we do know how to reason. And history is something that you live as well as something that you read about. I have lived this. I have paid attention.

One of the changes that I will talk about is the recent idea that the academic credentials that you "buy" from colleges determine what you are able to talk about with credibility. That is, what could I know about history if I don't have a college degree in History? What would qualify me to write a book if I don't have a college degree in Literature? How could I work on my car if I am not a union mechanic?

This thinking pigeon holes people based on their formal training. Yet history shows this to be completely false. Many great writers didn't even go to college, nor did many great mathematicians or music composers. Bill Gates does not have a degree in business. It is a recent notion, no doubt promulgated by those who sell academic credentials, that you are unqualified to speak outside your formal training. Yet these people at the same time tell us that they are educating people with a general education.

When I went to college I just wanted to take Math courses. Yet I was required to take courses in Literature, History, Science, Philosophy, and other things just get a college degree in Math. These same people might say that I am unqualified to write a book. I should have paid them more money and taken more literature courses if I wanted to write a book.

Well I was born at night but it was not last night. This is just one of the many things that I do not agree with. A book stands or falls on its own regardless of the academic credentials of the author. Words stand on their own. Music is the same way. Imagine that you hear a great piece of music. Then you found out that the composer was a fireman who never studied music in college. When heard again would it sound bad to you knowing that? I will discuss the economics of this thinking in later chapters. It is in fact all about income to credential sellers. What ever happened to "the proof of the pudding is in the eating" type of thinking.

When I started this book I began by writing the titles of the chapters on which I wanted to write. There were about 15 chapters. Then I wrote them. I assumed that I would expand them as I rewrote them. But I found on rewriting that I had said all that I wanted to say about that. I did not want to be repetitive and boring. I wanted to just discuss the essence of the issue even if that meant a short chapter. On that subject I had said all that I wanted to say. So if I wanted a thicker book I would have to add more chapters. I added about 12 chapters to the original table of contents as on each reading I thought of something else to talk about.

So read this book and pay attention to the words, to the thoughts and ask if you agree. Forget who wrote it. Words are magic, they have a life of their on regardless of where they come from.

I have been writing this book all my life. I wrote it while watching the nonsense on the 6 o'clock news. I wrote it while listening to the nonsense speeches of politicians running for office. I wrote it while trying to fall asleep at night thinking about my declining country. I wrote it while working with the self-serving bureaucrats in government and corporate America. I wrote it while teaching school. In short, I lived it and I wrote what I have lived.

In writing, you can assume that the reader will read the first sentence. That has to cause him to want to read the next sentence and the next. The first chapter must cause the reader to want to read the second chapter, and the next. If it does not work like this then the writer has failed and written a book that it is an effort to plow through and not a pleasure to read. I hope I have not failed.

This is a timely book since the 2010 and 2012 elections are approaching. It matters that you vote since the newly elected government has to be able to claim a mandate and that it is carrying out the will of the people. When the political body is split 50/50 as we now are, little can get accomplished and little progress can be made.

Chapter 1

The Two Americas

"Inequality has the natural necessary effect, under the present circumstances, of materializing our upper class, vulgarizing our middle class, and brutalizing our lower class" - Matthew Arnold

I chose the topic as the first chapter because this seems to be the end result of everything that has happened in America in the last 50 years.

When John Edwards ran for president he spoke of the two Americas. He was referring to the rich and the poor. This was a clear case of playing the class warfare card trying to get the support of the poor by playing them off against the rich. This cheap trick has been used before and typically by candidates who have no vision and no solutions for our problems.

But he was right. There are two Americas. He just misidentified them.

The first is a set of people who have a good salary, job security, automatic raises, health insurance, paid vacation, sick leave and a good pension when they retire. The second America is those people who have none of that. They make less money, often have no job security and are at the mercy of current economy's ups and downs, no health care in many cases, little to no paid vacations, little or no sick leave and in most cases no pension to retire on except social security.

The first America are all those who work for the government. This includes federal, state, county and city governments. This includes the military and police who will be called in to subdue Americans in times of civil unrest when Americans finally get fed up with all this, the teachers who are usually leftist and who are often brainwashing these young minds, all the bureaucrats who make all the regulations that control our lives and the IRS employees who collect taxes for pay for the first America.

By the way, taxes are collected at the point of a gun despite the fact that the government brags that we have the largest "volunteer" tax system in the world. Let's say that you don't pay your taxes. After many letters, the government will eventually put a tax lien on all your property. When they come to seize your home, car, your boat, your camper and everything else you have, he will be a federal marshal and he will be armed. If you resist the seizure violently the gun will come out at it will be pointed at you. Taxes are collected at the point of a gun. It's just that most people simply pay them to avoid the hassle but taxes will be collected at gun point if necessary.

The first America also includes the Congress and state legislatures who pass all these laws that we often object to. Also included are their staffers. It includes all city, county, state and federal employees who write and enforce the law.

Except for the military, all the people are in unions which protect them. These are called public sector unions and now there are more people in public sector unions than there are in all the other unions put together. They are forbidden to go on strike but they don't let a little thing like the law stop them. They are the law. Teachers have gone on strike and you may remember when the air traffic controllers went on strike. Fortunately Reagan was president and he simply fired them for breaking the law. A democrat president would have just given them more money.

When teachers go on strike the first demand is to be given legal immunity for breaking the law by going on strike. That is the first demand for even entering into talks to end the strike.

Secondarily, we can and should count all the employees who work for the defense industry because, even though they are not government employees, they get their salaries and benefits through government contracts. So they are, in fact, government employees, just indirectly This is true for all people who contract with the government to the extent that their company's income comes from federal, state, county and city government spending. This may be true for the man who picks up your garbage.

Will Rogers said that the hardest thing to recognize is a tax dollar on its way back from Washington. What we may say is it's hard to recognize who is really just another government employee.

Statistics show that those in the first America make a higher average salary than those in the second America and their pensions are higher. Furthermore, they will not have to participate in Obama's healthcare system.

So what about the second America? These are the people who compete in the rat race which is called the private sector. They have no guaranteed anything. When the first America screws up the economy, it's the second America that gets laid off.

Adding insult to injury, the second America pays for the first America with their taxes, ultimately collected at the point of a gun remember.

During the economic recovery underway, most of the jobs that have been created are government jobs. The first America certainly knows how to take care of itself.

This process can only end in revolution as history has shown. The Tea Party may be the first step - organizing the common people who are fed up with this. These Americans are being called radicals, extremists, angry mobs and racists (presumable because the President is black.) The Russian revolution began when a crowd gathered in front of the palace to present their concerns to the czar. This was a peaceful attempt to communicate with their government which ended when the palace guards drove them away, killing many in the process. Then the revolution began.

Great civil unrest has already occurred in America. You may remember the civil rights movement and the movement to end the Viet Nam war. Thousands of citizens showed up to petition their government for redress of grievances as the Constitution puts it and guarantees it as a right. Once in the anti war protests they were going to shut down the government.

They were going to do this peacefully by putting so many people on the bridges and major streets of D.C. that the city would become paralyzed. But, although the Constitution did not get into it, it turns out that you need to get a permit from the very government you are protesting to hold the protest. That permit can put conditions on the protest. They can limit you to where you can go or march to. They typically limit you to a certain part of town and let you vent. Here is how they look at. OK, let's let them march and wave their signs, vent their emotions and all this will be over in a couple of days, then we can go back to business as usual.

But the government was not about to let anybody shut down the government. It sets a bad example. It's poor form to let the citizens take control.

Once the anti-war protesters declared their intentions to march and close down Washington, the permit that was issued limited the marchers to certain bridges and streets and blocks of those streets. There would be no shutting down Washington. Of course, the threat was made that anyone who violates the terms of the permit would be arrested. (The government loves to threaten its citizens. It's exercising power without actually exercising power.). It's curious that a citizen threatening another citizen may be breaking the law depending on how it's done. It is often legal grounds for a court issued no contact order.

Well the kids were having none of that. They were romantic revolutionaries after all. And their thinking was that they can't arrest us all because there is not enough space in the jails to hold us all. They were naive despite, or maybe because of, the time they had spent in college. When the march began and when the permit was violated, they were arrested by the hundreds. But where were they detained? They were detained at the RFK stadium.

It turns out that a modern sport's stadium is the perfect place to detain large amount of people. They seat 50,000 people and you can cramp a few more thousand on the field. They have gates to assure that only ticket holders can get in and they have restrooms, which would be a necessity. The gates can be easily guarded to see that no one gets out. There would be no food but you are in prison after all and should suffer a little. Not eating for a few days will weaken you and make you easier to handle when you are released.

Well it turns out that every major city has one or more of these stadiums or what might be called "mass detention centers". So the government can easily handle mass riots all over the country.

Another thing I noticed in these marches was how cleverly the government was able to build barricades. Rope lines are not very effective in holding back an angry mob. What the government did in D.C. was to park city busses front to back in a line. They surrounded the White House with these bus barricades. This technique makes a perfect barricade. They are about eight feet high with smooth sides so that there is nothing to hold on to if you try to climb over them. They are low to the ground and you can barely get under them and it you do, you come out the other side on your stomach ready to be handcuffed and taken to the stadium. Parked front to back you can't get between them. It's perfect.

Furthermore, major cities, where a revolution would surely start, have thousands them, curiously bought by the federal government. So any major city can create impenetrable barricades for crowd control. Factor in the police departments and nation guard, America is well positioned to protect itself in case of civil unrest. Will people get killed? Sure, remember Kent State? But that is the cost of doing business.

So these are the two Americas and the way that the first America will protect itself from the second America.

.

Chapter 2

Conservatism vs. Liberalism

One cannot conceive anything so strange and so improbable that has not already been said by one philosopher or another" - Descartes

I decided that there is a need to briefly explaining conservatism and liberalism. Understanding this is necessary to the understanding, not only of this book, but of politics in general. Who are these Liberals and what do they believe? How do they differ from Conservatives?

First, the meaning of liberalism has changed complicating the situation. Our Founding Fathers were Liberals and believed in human freedom, thus the American Revolution. Liberals in those days were opposed to kings. They were opposed to dictators. Most people believed in human initiative and human freedom. Many did not even believe in a strong federal government. Thus, we began our country with the Articles of Confederation. The states were nearly sovereign countries with their own money, constitutions and governments. The Liberals today, under a new definition of liberalism, have come to believe in a strong central government and a big central government that dictates to everybody through government laws and regulations.

The biggest issue in forming our constitutional government was the issue of state's rights. Having lived under a king, everyone was afraid of a large, powerful central government. Section 8 of the Constitution lists the 18 specific powers that the Congress will have.

Article 9 reads "the enumeration in the Constitution of certain rights shall not be construed to deny or disparage others retained by the people." By this the Founding Fathers meant that the rights listed in the Bill of Rights are not the only rights that the people have. The government cannot say that these are your only rights. We have a right to change jobs, for example, and to travel freely around the country. In many countries, this requires government permission.

Article 10 reads "The powers not delegated to the United States by the Constitution, nor prohibited by it [the Constitution] to the states are reserved to the states respectively or to the people." This means that any powers not specifically given to the federal government by the Constitution belong to the states.

For example, states have the power to define the laws under which people get married. They define the probate laws that distribute property to one's heirs after death. They define criminal laws concerning theft, murder and the like. These laws vary greatly from state to state. States then were generally thought to be separate countries and intended by the Founding Fathers to function nearly as separate countries, except that, among other things, they could not sign treaties and make war.

So what happened? How did the federal government get so big and become so intrusive into our lives? Originally, there were the Department of State, the Department of War, the Department of Treasury, Department of Justice (Attorney General), and Postmaster General. President Washington had 5 members in his cabinet. Today there are 15 members in the president's cabinet. These departments cover nearly every aspect of life.

Well, first there is a disagreement between Conservatives and Liberals about the Constitution itself. The Conservatives think that the Constitution is an anchor that holds us to a certain behavior regarding the government and its role in governing the people. It is fixed and to be translated literally. The Liberals, on the other hand, don't see any reason that we should be held absolutely to something that was written two centuries ago by people of a different time and a different age. They think that the Constitution should be a living document and be able to grow with the times and the needs of the people. Our needs are different than the needs of the people in 1789.

This is a fundamental difference in thinking. The Founding fathers realized this and put into the Constitution, a way to amend it if things changed. The problem is that the Constitution was made difficult to amend and on purpose. To amend the Constitution, under Article 5, is takes 2/3 of both houses of Congress and then the amendment has to be ratified by 3/4 of the state legislatures. Notice that the President plays no role in amending the Constitution other than perhaps suggesting an amendment. In the early 70's President Johnson championed the 26 amendment allowing 18 year olds to vote. Amending the Constitution is so hard to do, this has only happened 27 times in our history.

But the whole point of a Constitution is to set forth a set of principles that become the basis of law. The idea of a living constitution is, in fact, an oxymoron. Imagine a ship's anchor that floats. How will the ship be held in place? The ship will wander to where ever the current takes it. If our Constitution can easily be changed then we float and drift with the attitudes of the time. This is what the Declaration of Independence calls "light and transient causes." It says that governments long established should not be changed for light and transient causes.

This gives the Liberals a problem. If they believe in a living constitution, then how do they make it live, given how hard it is to amend it. This is not a problem for the Conservatives because they think that it is fixed, works and needs little amending.

Thus the Liberals see the courts as the way to change the Constitution through interpretation. This makes control of the Supreme Court a paramount political issue today. In the end, all you have to control is the Supreme Court. The courts fiddling with the Constitution through interpretation has given rise to the concept of "activist judges". This fiddling has allowed more and more intrusion into our lives by the federal government and curtailed states rights in the process.

The process used is to assert that the rights given to the people by the Constitution cannot be reduced by state law. This is true. The problem arises in interpreting the rights given to the people by the Constitution.

Recently a case went to the Washington DC federal appeals court about Washington DC's law restricting guns in the city. The court ruled that the 2nd amendment guarantees the right of citizens to bear arms even in cities that try to ban them. This went to the Supreme Court in D.C vs. Heller. The high court said that Washington D.C. could not pass a law preventing its citizens from having a gun. It violates the 2nd amendment. Conservatives around the country agreed, Liberals disagreed.

But the Supreme Court also ruled that there is an implied right to privacy in the Constitution so women had a right to have their fetus aborted in private by their doctor. This stuck down any laws that might exist in the states preventing abortion. Conservatives disagreed, Liberals agreed.

Government intrusion into our lives usually increases the size of government.

Now we come to the second difference between Liberals and Conservatives today, a living constitution being the first.

Conservatives today believe in a small central government with fewer regulations controlling people's lives while the Liberals tend to support a big federal government with many regulations. Yet Liberals are always talking about personal freedom which is difficult to achieve under a plethora of government regulations.

Conservatives believe in a set of rules by which one should live. These usually include the 10 Commandments and often the teachings of Christ. They include rules on etiquette and rules on general social behavior. Liberals see these rules as limiting personal freedom. "Why can't I behave as I wish as long as I am not hurting anyone else?" Well because you are setting a bad example to those who are watching you, especially young people who may look to you for their example. Second, you may be hurting yourself and when you fail, then you will be looking to us for help usually in the form of money. When you become a burden to society then it is no longer your business. These rules are about having a successful life and have been developed over thousands of years - rules that work. If you want to go off in the woods and live by yourself like an animal then you can do what you wish. But if you want to live in society with civilized people, then there are certain rules which we all follow and you are expected to follow them too. And you will have to give up some degree of what you choose to call personal freedom.

The big government comes chiefly from social programs. This leads to another difference between Liberals and Conservatives. Conservatives see a nation where everybody has a fair share but not the fair share that Liberals speak of. Conservatives think that your fair share is your free 12 year education. Everyone has access to one and there you can learn the skills that you will need to make a living and support yourself. You learn to read and write English, learn math and science, learn history, learn computers and more. Do it right and you even have a chance to go to college. Make good grades and you can get a scholarship. Most people in the world do not have this chance. They go into the fields by age 7. Many never have a chance in life. So take your fair share and enjoy your life.

To the Liberals fair share is more about a fair outcomes. There will be people who will not take advantage of their free education and will be poor. To the liberal this is an unfair outcome. They have a long list of excuses for why people fail. Conspicuously absent from that list are the individuals themselves and their behavior. To the liberal it's all the society's fault that people fail at life and therefore, society should help. Thus, the social programs that lead a big central government.

Sometimes given the clever name of "safety nets", these government programs make these individuals dependent on government and thus dependent on the Liberals. This is a ready-made political constituency. Just keep us in power and everything will be OK is the call. Now there are people who need help in life. The disabled, the sick, the old and infirmed, and the mentally ill are among these. Everyone agrees that we should help these people.

The Liberals, generally Democrats, represent people who do not understand many things like most political and economic issues being addressed here. To appeal to people who do not understand these things, the Democrats have to resort to clever sayings. There was the New Deal, the New Frontier, the Great Society and terms like a "fair share", and "livable wage". What is a livable wage? Well that depends on how you want to live. If you want to drive a car, have cable TV, eat prepared food, and dress well, it will take more money. If you want to ride public transportation, prepare meals from raw food, and listen to the radio, it will take less money. So what is needed is a definition for what is an acceptable life style for the poor then a livable wage can be calculated. Yet we see no such standard being proposed and for obvious reasons. No politicians are going to say that the poor do not need to drive a car and have cable TV. The first people who would object to this thinking would be the businessmen who make TVs and cars - usually Republicans. Thus it is in the interest of politicians from both parties that welfare continue, but not in the interest of the taxpayer.

The same is true for the term "fair share". What is that? Is that a certain amount of money? How much? Most people's state in life is because of the decisions they have made. Bad decisions lead to a hard life. The government can't make everyone's decisions for them.

In summary Conservatives see a world that requires individual initiative and individual responsibility while Liberals see a world where votes can be had by making people dependent on government. This is a major difference in outlooks.

When you have big government, you of necessity have high taxes. Somebody has to pay for this. There are several ways to tax. The flat tax would tax everyone, say, $5000 an year. That is what it would cost to live in America. This is the only form of equal taxation. The flat tax rate would tax everyone, say 20% of their salary a year. This is not equal taxation since different people would pay more or less money to live in America. But this seems fair to those who support it. The variable tax rate would tax people at a different rate depending on their income. Those making more money would pay higher tax rates than those who have less income. Many think that this in unfair. It penalizes the successful. Since successful people are what you want, why penalize them? It's not like they did not work for what they have. They studied in school, went on to college and worked hard to be successful.

The call from the Liberals is to tax the rich more using a curious rationale. America has been good to them so they should pay more in taxes. America is a country. It is not good or bad to any body. It does not have a will nor play favorites. It's an environment where you take your fair share education and with your good or bad decisions, make the best of your life.

But there are fortunate ones. These are the people who inherit great fortunes with out having to work for them. Thus, there is a call for an inheritance tax and there is one. Then there are luxury taxes that tax certain products that you buy. What you buy is a matter of your own personal freedom to spend your money. Why should you pay an extra tax on a diamond ring and not on a car? This too is a way of taxing those awful rich people.

Conservatives tend to believe in something like a flat tax rate and little taxation. Most Liberals tend to believe in taxing the rich to support social programs for the poor.

Conservatives think that the poor are people who did not take advantage of their fair share education and made bad decisions all their lives. Conservatives are willing to help those who are trying to help themselves.

Liberals say that these people came from broken homes and from parents who themselves have no education. They do not motivate their children. Well what can we do about that? How can society fix that? We can take their children away from them and put the children in orphanages. Nobody would sit still for that. We can try to convince the children that their parents are wrong so don't listen to your parents. Here is how you should be, this is what you should think. Society, especially the bad parents, are not going to sit still for that either. We, that is, society, do not intrude into the family. So we can't fix it. This is both why poverty is generational and why a war on poverty will fail. A war on poverty can never get to the root causes of poverty apart from offering a public school system.

Still another difference between Conservatives and Liberals is how much control the government should have over the economy. Conservatives want an economy free of government control where the marketplace makes the decisions. Liberals want a centrally controlled economy where bureaucrats make the decisions. They argue that the economy is too important to be left to chance. Educated people should make these economic decisions. The problem with that approach is that economic decisions immediately become politicized. If a sector of the economy is failing because people are not buying their products or services, then Liberals rush in to help and to help those people stay employed. Perhaps we can give a tax break to people to encourage them to buy from that industry. Perhaps we, the government, can buy those products and services and stockpile them or give them to the poor as they once did with cheese.

Conservatives would tend to say that perhaps the economy is changing and those products are no longer needed. Perhaps those products have been replaced with other technologies. Let the economy adjust to this. The people will find other work. This, admittedly sounds cruel but that is how free economies have always worked. That is why we have few buggy whip manufacturers today and few blacksmiths.

So there are significant differences in the thinking of Liberals and Conservatives and thus Republicans and Democrats. People who think that it does not matter who I vote for because nothing is going to change are dead wrong. There are two entirely different possible societies that we can live in. One is a free society where people are responsible for their own lives and individual initiative and personal responsibility are paramount. The other is a society run by big government with all the attendant regulations and high taxes where people

are "taken care of" by the government. Which society we live in is totally up to who is in power for most of the time.
.

Chapter 3

The Body Politic

"Don't tell my mother I'm in politics. She thinks I play the piano in a whorehouse." - Anonymous

There are about 511,000 elected officials in America. Our problems are not for a lack of elected officials in our democracy. This number includes not only legislators and governors, but school boards, judges, and dog catchers. One thing to remember about how we elect our leaders is that it has been a dirty business from the beginning. As bad as the system looks today, it's historically typical. The election of Thomas Jefferson was perhaps the dirtiest in history. Entire books have been written about it.

A grand change between the election system designed by our Founding Fathers and what we have today is in the number and kind of voter. The Founding Fathers designed a system where white, male, property owners voted. Women played little role in the business of government in those days. The feeling was that all women got married and the husband, as head of the family, represented the family's interests with his vote. Also, there was no income tax. The federal government got its money by taxing exports and imports at the major ports. States got their money chiefly through property taxes. Since property owners paid these property taxes they should have a say in the government that taxed them.

Limiting voters to property owners was accomplished by the poll tax. Anyone who could afford it could vote even if they did not own property and some non-property owners did vote. So the voters, it was thought, were educated men (property owners) who had a financial interest in the laws being passed and so they would be conscientious with their valuable vote.

The first major change in this system was after the Civil War when black men got the right to vote. Later, during the women's suffrage movement, women, including black women, got the right to vote. Then in the 60's President Lyndon Johnson got the voting age reduced from age 21 to age 18. The thinking was if they were old enough to be drafted and sent to war, they should have the vote and knowing that they would vote liberal.

Now some want to extend the vote to convicted felons, who are prohibited from voting, and now we hear that illegal immigrants are voting. Extending the vote is done by politicians and given to citizens that would vote for them. The Republicans after the Civil War assumed that the Blacks would vote for the Republicans who liberated them. Lyndon Johnson assumed that the idealistic young people would vote Democratic. Those who are trying to get the vote extended to felons, the Liberals, assume that these convicted felons will vote for the Democrats, as will any illegal immigrants since many need the social services that the Left provides. I am not saying that universal suffrage is bad, I am merely explaining its effect on the body politic. But what argument would you may against extending the vote to 16 year olds? Many work and pay taxes. This is taxation without representation, a phrase that started the American Revolution. The English made a big mistake by not simply giving the Americans a few seats in the House of Commons, eh?

Although the Hispanic vote is split about 60/40 – democrat/republican – there is a race to get the Hispanic vote. Neither side wants to be seen as anti-Hispanic by insisting on a fence along the border for example. Other ways to lose the Hispanic vote is to support the idea of English as the official language, support ending bilingual education in schools, support ending welfare for illegal immigrants, support stopping children of illegal immigrants for attending public schools, insisting on employers being fined for hiring illegals and support ending sanctuary cities where illegals can live without fear that the local police will report them to the federal government. Support any of this and you lose the Hispanic vote or at least a majority of it. In these days of close elections, neither party can afford this. This explains the mystery of why we have allowed ourselves to be invaded by 12 million Mexicans. Note that this would not have happened in with the system original designed by the Founding Fathers.

Another change in the body politic is how much power a very small minority of voters have with America split about 51% to 49%, liberal and conservative. A good example of this is the gay vote. Gays are a very small percentage of the population. Yet, these days, their vote can swing a close election. Thus, nobody wants to alienate the gays. Thus, they have great power. Power beyond their numbers. The Jews are in the same position. This power comes from the fact that these minority groups are willing to vote as a bloc. However, as the pendulum swings to say a 60% to 40% either way, all this power evaporates. Everyone realizes this so that when the moment is right, as it is now, these things have to be locked into law. Things like gay marriage.

As people, the huddled masses, who have no idea what is going on in terms of international affairs and national economics, to name two, vote, then on what do they base their vote? They vote based on how well they like the candidate. Thus, being liked becomes the trait that modern politicians seek. These people are generally attractive and have charisma. TV adds to the idea of star quality as a qualification for getting elected. Thus, money is needed to buy the expensive TV time.

Therefore, the role that money plays in the process has increased. Early elections featured news paper articles and printed pamphlets. That did not cost a lot of money. But elections ride on the back of technology. When the railroads came into being, whistle stop tours became the way to run for President. Making speeches from the back of the last car as the train stopped at every little town cost more money to pay for the train.

Later radio was invented and still more money was needed to buy time on the radio to get the message out. That cost even more money. Finally came the 800 pound gorilla – television. Sixty seconds of television time costs thousands of dollars. Running your message several times a night on prime time for months of an election season costs millions of dollars.

Thus we have an electorate, who has no clue as to what the real issues and vote based on star quality, appearance and charisma. Fashion specialists choose the apparel. Makeup artists make the candidate attractive, professional speech writers tell them what to say and body language experts tell them how to move. It is exactly what goes on in Hollywood when making a movie. And like a movie, you can have many takes. The idea is to make many takes and figure our later which take to put on TV.

Speaking of makeup, the people who heard the Kennedy/Nixon debates on the radio thought that Nixon won. Those who saw it on TV thought that Kennedy won.

The political message, too, is undergoing change. George Orwell showed his genius when he addresses this is his famous book 1984. He coined the word "newspeak". He realized that points could be made and arguments could be won if you could just change the meaning of words. For example, the word "family" used to refer to a dad, a mom and a couple of kids. Now the meaning of that word is being changed. For example, we are being told that two gay men living together is a family. Taken to extremes, any group of people living under the same roof with a loosely connected economic situation is a family. This means that wherever the word "family" is used in the law, it applies to these families also. This naturally changes the meaning of the phrase "family values". What are family values in the context of these new families?

Any lifestyle can now be justified by calling it an "alternative lifestyle". Sodomites are now called gay. Much of this is done under the doctrine of "political correctness". In its beginning it made some sense. For example, we should not call fat people fat, we should say that they are obese. This was more a matter of manners at that point. But there is always another shoe to fall. The question always is where are they going with this?

Taken to extremes it's speech control. There might soon be a list of words that one can't use in public discourse. It might be considered as "hate speech". First, we make hate speech against the law, then we are obligated to issue a list of hate speech words. Speech control at its finest.

Politicians, or at least their speech writers, are attuned to this. Speeches are carefully written to avoid any words on the list that are not politically correct. Mark Twain said that the difference between the right word and almost the right word is like the difference between lightning and lightning bug. He was right. Nothing works like he right word. But what if the right word is on the list of politically incorrect words?

All of this has the effect of eliminating straight talk, despite John McCain's "straight talk express", and watering down political speech into meaningless words which when put together with the right hand gestures, makes it look like something worthwhile was just said. Factor in a good looking person with the right clothes and makeup and you have a candidate for office.

Today it is generally accepted that politicians should be lawyers and have experience. Have you ever wondered what the background of those who signed the Declaration of Independence was? Of the 56, 24 were lawyers and jurists. 11 were merchants, 9 were farmers and large plantation owners. I wonder if the Founding Fathers felt that all politicians should be lawyers.

They do write laws after all but every committee has staff lawyers available for that work. So the legislators on the committee could be businessmen, teachers, farmers, doctors, etc. In fact, and most American do not know this, but much legislation is written be the lobbyists themselves. They present the bill they wrote, usually hundreds of pages, to the committee and say that this is the bill that we would like to see passed by Congress. So in many cases they write the bill and provide it in machine readable form as well.

The other, and perhaps more alarming dimension to a candidate's resume, is that he or she must have experience in politics. This creates the "professional politician." Now what is a professional politician? What traits does he or she have? Well, there is experience in government. They have been around. They have many friends and contacts. But can only such people write and get good laws passed? Do people vote for legislation out of friendship instead of the words in the proposed law? Hopefully not, so why would the number of friends they have matter.

As for experience in government there are hearings where people come forward to talk about the issues in the proposed law. These people have experience too. It's their job to educate the committee members.

All this tends to keep ordinary people out of politics because the public has bought into the idea that what we need are professional politicians who can bring back the pork from

Washington. Well, we need only to look around to see the mess that these professional politicians have made.

One can judge people by the people that they elect to office. People vary across America, some sophisticated and some not too sophisticated. The politicians they elect to office are a mirror reflection of the electorate who put them there. One sees some congressmen who are, shall we say, not Churchill's. Accordingly, one sees politicians who speak correctly, use sophisticated sentences and say something significant. Seeing the part of the country that they come from explains this phenomenon.

Many of the changes in politics is due to the idea of diversity. We were told in the 70's and 80's that diversity was good, diversity is American's strength. It is a natural thing to say when you find yourself diverse. The psychologists call this the "sweet lemons" rational. Stuck with something, you rational that it is a good thing to have.

The idea quickly grew. If diversity is good, then more diversity is better. This has many handy uses. The influx of illegal Mexicans makes us more diverse. H1B visas used to bring in the technical workers that our failing education system can't produce makes us more diverse. Thus, all this is good.

There is an active effort to make college campuses more diverse. Apparently, a campus of white males would fail as an education institution despite the fact that the Georgia Institute of Technology produced many fine engineers for many years as a chiefly male institution. West Point produced fine officers. There are even all women's campuses. They worked as well.

What is behind this is that the function of schools has changed. They now produce well rounded citizens rather than mere educated people. We see this is high school as well now being highly socialized but producing kids who can't do math.

It is in fact that schools, an arm of the state, are attempting to create what it thinks are well-rounded citizens. This is a dangerous process.

Diversity has changed the political discourse in two ways. First, politicians have to appeal to people of many cultures and second, the issues become more complex requiring some fancy dancing to work around. We are no longer a melting pot but a mosaic. Mosaic societies do not have their own culture, rather they are a blend of many cultures.

The first round of large scale immigration in the late 19th century was from Europe and they had no problem blending in. This latest immigration movement is by people from Asia and the Middle East. Asians are not interested in immigrating to America to become Europeanized. They want to maintain their own culture. In earlier days, there were efforts to teach everyone English. Today, the trend is to have bi-lingual education.

These people have different cultures and religions. Suppose there is something in their culture that we find offensive in our culture like female circumcision. What happens next? Do we allow it because it's part of their culture although it might actually be illegal here? Suppose their culture allows what we would call under age drinking. Suppose their culture allows drug use. Suppose their culture allows a man to beat his wife. Many cultures do.

If our laws trump their culture, a case could be made that our laws discriminate against their culture and by extension discriminates against them. Since laws can't discriminate, what do we do now?

We never saw an argument that diversity was good. We were just suppose to accept it as, as self-evident. Diversity, in fact, factionalizes society and the common interest becomes harder to define.

Cultural discrimination will be the next great social issue in America, replacing racial and gender discrimination.

We see this now with the language issue. With more and more with Spanish speaking citizens there is an effort to teach kids in Spanish. There is also a reactionary effort to make English the official language. Anybody for that are called anti-Hispanic and even racist and are sure to lose the Hispanic vote.

Many businesses phone lines say "for English press 1, para Espanol markque dos." They want the Hispanics to know that their money is welcomed. Businesses don't care about politics, they only care about money. Businesses will kowtow to anybody. The bowing is insincere to be sure but it makes money. The customer is always right, even when they are wrong.

We never had this problem to this degree in the first wave of immigration and everyone learned English. Other minority groups are insisting on using their own language. Driver's license applications, voting material and other government documents are now available in Spanish and other languages at an extra cost to the taxpayer.

The problem with all this is that America is an English speaking country and the sooner you learn it and the better you can speak it, the better are your chances for getting ahead and becoming prosperous. Imagine that you went to China and spoke little Chinese. Would anyone hire you? You would not even be able to communicate effectively with your co-workers. Nobody would give you a job, nor could you go to school.

This is the predicament that many Hispanics and others will find themselves in in the future, all along claiming some sort of discrimination. The politicians seeking their vote will be supporting them just like they did with the bilingual education issue. Not finding gainful employment, many will turn to welfare. Of course, at the welfare office, employees will be expected to speak Spanish, for example. In fact, that could be a prerequisite for getting the job. So then we have this absurd situation. An American can't get a government job which their tax dollars pay for because he or she can only speak their native language, English.

We are doing Hispanics and all other minority groups a great disservice by not forcing them to learn English. They will not understand the contracts that they are signing. They will be a sucker class for any clever businessman that wants to take advantage of them. Maybe that's the point. Maybe this is class warfare. Maybe the point is to create a class that can be taken advantage of by businessmen and politicians.

Today, the Left controls the national press, the school systems, the colleges and universities, and Hollywood. Their social agenda is being taught in elementary and high schools, and to a lesser extent in universities. It is to a lesser extent because in college, students can often pick their college professors, students in lower schools can not pick their teachers.

The Left's effect from Hollywood is not so much that movies carry a Liberal message, though some do, but rather because actors become famous. Being famous they can get on TV and speak to the public. This represents a major change from the Hollywood of the past. Earlier, studios specifically told their actors and actresses not to take political stands in public. The idea was that this was sure to alienate some fans. But that was when the studio system pervaded Hollywood and movie making. Studios spent great sums of money grooming and fashioning their stars because the star was the drawing card for movie attendance.

But the studio system is largely gone. Stars are no longer under contract to a studio and obliged to obey the rules that the studio sets forth in the contract. Stars are more like free agents and free to speak their mind. So we see them at rallies denouncing the war, denouncing President Bush and publicly supporting the candidate of their choice. There is nothing wrong with this except that the public can't get past the star quality to ask "what are his or her credentials to take this position." For example, what does this star know about the military? Has he/she ever been in the military? Has he/she ever been to Iraq. Have they ever read a book about the history of the Middle East in general and Iraqi history specifically? Where did they get the information to take a public position on the war and try to influence public opinion? But these questions are never asked as the public is blinded by star quality.

So Hollywood actors are influencing public opinion and their opinions are generally Leftist. How did they come to be Liberals. You would think that they had a hard life climbing to the top in a highly competitive field. You would think that they spent a lot of time unemployed or working menial jobs. The joke in L.A. is when you meet someone who says he/she is an actor, you ask them what restaurant they work at.

They have worked hard but many of their views come from the businessmen with whom they have to sign contracts. They come to loath these businessmen, who try to cheat them at every turn. And by extension, they come to loath all businessmen. Well, since most businessmen are Republicans then that loathing extends to Republicans as well.

But there is a compensating angle. Actors are good looking people. They have to be. It's part of star quality. It is an unfortunate fact of life that beautiful people have it easier in life. Beautiful women can open doors with just a smile.

Handsome men turn eyes and get attention wherever they go. So their lives are not all that hard when compared to people who are not attractive. I suspect that they have had it easy and thus tend to be liberal in their thinking. Often, how hard you have to work at life depends on how cute you are.

Finally, they tend to appeal to the politics of their fans. Most movie goers are young and not yet hardened by life, thus they tend to be liberal, and most movie goers are in the liberal big cities. Small towns are lucky to have one movie theater while big cities have a dozen movie theaters.

So Hollywood is typically liberal and the stars can easily get before the public and express their liberal views to a candid public who seldom wonders where they get the authority to speak on those subjects.

But to their credit they do get involved which is more than can be said for most people. Only about half the public even votes and fewer still attend school board meetings and city council meetings. Fewer still write editorials for their local newspapers. So we have to admire people who get involved even if we disagree with their position on matters. At least they are involved.

The annoying thing for me about Hollywood is their remaking of great movies. Often this is done to upgrade the movie to a newer technology but too often they change the message of the original movie. It that case, it can become George Orwell's history rewrite come true. The problem is that the viewer did not see the version of twenty years ago to be able to compare the message of original with the message of the remake. They only see the remake and its message. And older viewers who might remember the original movie don't tend to go to the movies as much as younger people do, especially if they saw the original. So the process is ripe for rewriting history to the extent that movies represent history at all. Hollywood is famous for departing from the facts to make a more entertaining movie.

The problem is that many people don't distinguish between movies and TV and reality. They assume that what they see in the movies and on TV is reality. They think that this is the way the world actually works. Of course there is justice, just watch Law and Order. The criminal always gets caught and punished. In reality few criminals are caught and those who are often plea bargain down the offense and might get only probation or jail time and early release.

When crimes are reported on the news the crime itself is news. If they catch the criminal, that is news also. What is not news is what eventually happens to the criminal. Have you even wondered what happens to all those drivers you see on TV in those high speed chases. The chase is news. So did the guy go to jail, lose his license or what? Well that is never reported. I suspect little happens to these people but I do not know for sure because it is never reported.

Our evening news starts out with murders, rapes, robberies and the like. We are often 15 minutes into the news before non-crime stories are reported.

Recall that the press is generally Leftist and in a following chapter, I will make the assertion that the trail lawyers, who contribute heavily to the Democratic party, make more money if there are more criminals on the street. So with the press' support, nobody is made aware of the leniency with which these criminals are treated. That might expose the whole game. If you want to know what happens to criminals, watch Law and Order. It is not in the interest of the Liberals, supported by the trial lawyers, to let the public know what actually happened to these criminals. And the liberal press cooperates.

Another dimension to the body politic is the revolving door. This is where a politician loses the election so what now. He or she needs a job and they have resources – they know people on Capital Hill where they have served, for example. But this is true for local governments as well. So they become lobbyists. There is nothing wrong with lobbying and the Constitution allows us to "petition the government for redress of grievances". This is the legal foundation for lobbying.

The problem for any citizen wanting to talk to their representative or senator is access. How do you get in to see them? They are very busy with committee hearings and the like so the best most can do is speak with a legislative assistant. Perhaps your message will get through to his boss and perhaps it won't. It would be nice to speak with the legislator directly but that is difficult, difficult unless you know him or her because you used to serve with him or her when you were in office. Then you may be allowed access.

If you are to become an effective lobbyist you must have access to powerful people. So with the revolving door, defeated politicians become lobbyists because they have access to the legislators with whom they used to serve. You then charge clients money to get their message to the legislator through you. You will make their case for them. Why can't they make their own case? - because they do not have access.

What makes this process particularly disturbing is that these lobbyists often have clients who represent foreign governments and foreign companies who are competing with American companies. Imagine a powerful Senator is defeated, becomes a lobbyist and takes as a client a foreign company. His client may be competing with an American company for business or favorable legislation to make it easier to do business in America.

So now we have an American, formally a powerful senator, with many friends on Capital Hill, working for the interests of a foreign company and against the interests of an American company. You might think that a powerful American would support the interest of an American company but you would be wrong.

What he is actually doing as a lobbyist is working in his or her own selfish interest. He/she is making money working against the interests of American companies and getting paid a lot of money for that. There are also foreign lobbyists who lobby American politicians. Why would the legislator even meet with a foreign lobbyist? Well perhaps his company does business in America and pays taxes here. That makes the foreign company a taxpayer and the legislator feels an obligation to talk to all taxpayers, including foreign companies.

Yet another change in politics and an indication of how vicious the process is becoming is the tactic of shouting down a speaker. We value free speech in American and believe that everyone should be able to speak his or her mind. Yet we find all too often that the speaker is shouted down by hecklers in the audience. Typically, these are conservative speakers thus the hecklers would be Liberals. Yes, Liberals who profess to believe in freedom.

Many times conservative speakers are invited to a college or university to speak. Then they are shouted down, sometimes the stage is rushed and a spectacle is made of the entire appearance of the conservative. This comes, from of all places, colleges and universities which claim and even brag about being bastions of open learning, freedom and free speech. Yet the university officials do little to stop it. But then the officials are Liberals also.

Many think this is a planned ambush. We invite this conservative speaker here to speak. Then they are shouted down by the students making a spectacle of the conservative and the press is filming. Others see the invitation as sincere and it's just the students that do the dirty work. Whatever the cause and especially at a college or university, it should not be tolerated. The misbehaving students should simply be expelled for the quarter or semester for violating the civil rights of the speaker. In public rallies this would be harder to do since the protesters are on public property and are themselves exercising their own rights to free speech and freedom to assemble. But on campuses a case could be made to stop it.

The point is why is it happening? If I knew I was right and the speaker was wrong then I would let them speak. Then I will speak and we let the audience decide. But disrupting free speech you are sending the message that you are afraid of their words and by extension afraid that they are right and that the audience will agree with them. That is not a good message to send especially at a supposed place of education and enlightenment.

Another problem for democracies is there inability to plan. The party in power makes plans but if and when they are turned out of power, the new party cancels those plans and makes plans of their own. In effect over a, say, 20 years period there is no planning and no plans at all.

Realizing that the members of the House of Representatives would change every two years, and that this would result in a unstable government where hot legislation would be passed that addresses what the Founding Fathers called "light and transient causes", they established the Senate to add stability. The Senate typically represents the status quo while the House represents change. Often a bill will pass the House but not the Senate and visa versa. The Senate, which usually represents the interests of the rich becomes an anchor resisting changes that the people want.

Our political system does offer many ways for the public to be a part of the system. People can vote, contribute money to candidates, attend school board and city council meetings, write to Congress and other political offices, write editorials to the local paper and attend rallies and protests. Few citizens do these things and only about 50% even vote. Thus, it is said that people get the government that they deserve and by extension, they get the society that they deserve.

What we have is a disconnect in thinking. The public thinks, OK we put you into office so run things and don't bother me. The politicians are thinking, OK here we are in office so what do you want us to do? The public fails to consider that electing them is only the first step and that they must continually put pressure on the elected officials to do something. Meanwhile, the elected officials are saying that we don't hear any public outcry for these changes. To the public the thinking is that surly you can see what needs to be fixed unless you are blind. The elected officials are thinking that we represent the public's wishes. We are not dictators who just come up with these things on our own. Tell us what you want us to do. Meanwhile, the public is disengaged having elected people to run things.

We often hear things being called un-American. Now what is that? Are there things that are un-French, un-English or un-German? When the Beatles appeared in America their haircuts were called un-American. This caused the witty John Lennon to remark "That's very observant of them because we aren't American"

The name implies that America is somehow better and more than just an ordinary country and as such there are things that are un-American. What is it about America that makes us different in that sense? The world probably thinks that it is very pompous of us to use that term.

Finally, technology has changed to body politic, it is a property of statistics that a small sample of the population, if chosen randomly, will reflect the properties of the entire population. This means that if you choose 1000 people at random and ask them questions about something, their answers will reflect how the population of, say, one million people would answer those question. This is very convenient since it would be a lot of work to ask those million people something. In this example, a thousand times more work.

This feature of statistics has led to polling. If you want to see what 200,000,000 Americans are thinking, you need only to ask, say, 2000 American chosen at random. The more you ask, the smaller be what is called the margin of error in the poll. Polls are usually have a margin of error of 3 or 4 percentage points. This is because the pool of respondents is not truly random but as random as you can get it.

How has this affected politics? Well it lets the politicians know what the people are thinking about various issues and thus lets the politician know what to say in speeches when addressing the people. Is there anything wrong with that? The politician is, after all, supposed to be representing the people. By the polls, the politician knows what the people think.

But these people call themselves national "leaders" and not national "representatives". There is no leadership when you are simply voting the will of the people. The people may be wrong in their views. Who is going to change their mind? Somebody needs to be saying that this is what we should do or even this is what we must do and not just go along with the will of the people as shown by polls.

President Lyndon Johnson offered this kind of leadership during the civil right's movement. President Abraham Lincoln offered this kind of leadership during the Civil War. Who is offering this kind of leadership today and who is just reflecting the answers to questions in a poll?

Polls are often criticized by the way that the questions are asked. The wording of the question can often prejudice the answer that will be given. Then the pollster can claim something that the public does not actually think. Politicians who only pay attention to the polls are then misled.

This prejudicing of the answer leads to conflicting polls. Another way to prejudice a poll is by not using the random sample that is required for the validity of the poll. Suppose you conduct a poll in major U.S. cities. Then you claim that Americans believe this. No. All we can say that people who live in major cities believe this. In fact, if the major cities are all located in a particular geographic region of the country, then perhaps all you can say is that people in the South believe this or that or even that people who live in major cities in the South believe this of that.

It is important that the people understand the point that I am making here because this is how the system really works. This may be different from what they were taught in school.

Chapter 4

Lawyers and the Court System

"I do not care to speak ill of any man behind his back, but I believe the gentleman is an attorney" - Samuel Johnson

It must be well understood that a dead animal rots all over at the same time. Thus, in a society that is in decline, all the institutions will begin to fail. As our education system is failing so is our justice system. And as you read this book you will understand that all our institutions are failing.

We, as did the Romans, once had the best justice system in the world. But fundamental changes in the system took place. The first to be discussed and perhaps the most important is the idea of "activist judges. Although judges do not make law directly, their interpretations of existing law can have that effect.

For example, the Constitution reads in article 1 "Congress shall make no law respecting an establishment of religion …". So let's play with these words in the way that an activist judge might do. First by "Congress" they obviously meant the "government" so it actually reads "the Government shall make no law …". But it also can not be done by regulation, policy, etc. So it reads "The government shall make no law, regulation or policy, respecting an establishment of religion … ". But surely this extends beyond the federal government. For example, a state government can't do this either. It would make no sense to forbid the federal government to respect an establishment of religion and then allow the states to do it. Imagine if in a particular state, everybody had to be Catholic. But beyond states this certainly extends to county and city governments as well.

So now what we have is "Governments, federal, state and local shall make no law, regulation or policy respecting an establishment of religion ..." Now that sounds like a good thing. Well guess what? Schools are an arm of state government and allowing Christmas trees, nativity scenes, prayer and pictures of Jesus in schools is respecting Christianity. Also, nativity scenes on city hall grounds does the same. Therefore, all these are banned. Notice that no law was passed to ban Christmas from schools. Such a law would have never passed any legislature. Therefore, it had to be done by judicial edict, done by people who were not elected and responsible to no one. This is judicial activism at its finest.

In the last 40 years political parties, particularly the Left, realized that if they controlled the courts, they could get interpreted law in place that would bypass the legislative process. This results in laws that would have never passed the Congress or state legislatures. Another example is abortion. Abortion was made legal, not by the Congress and not by the state legislatures but by the Supreme Court. Indeed, control of that court is now the supreme fight going on in Washington D.C. today. The only question that is focused on at Senate hearings before the judicial committee is "do you support Roe vs. Wade?" That issue outweighs everything else.

And how was this done? By "inventing" a right to privacy in the Constitution. The word privacy does not even appear in the Constitution but the court said that it is there by implication. One might understand the privacy between the doctor and the patience. But in abortion clinics many people are around. Nurses, secretaries arranging the schedule, the billing people are all involved. That is not privacy between the doctor and the patient.

But judicial activist goes beyond the Supreme Court at least below it. Judicial activism exists in the lower federal courts.

California has an initiative process. The citizens can get something on the ballot as an initiative and have it voted on as law. This is democracy at its purist form. Many initiatives have been passed and the next step is always that somebody, the losers, files a law suit and issue goes to court. They are generally overturned in the courts, that is, by the courts, and that is the end of the people's will. For this to work, you have to have control of the courts. It is said the elections finalize or end something but in California, elections start something – a court fight.

Federal judges are nominated by the President and approved by the Senate. This means if you have control of the Presidency and the Senate you can stack the courts with people favorable to your socio-political position. Then you simply take everything to the federal courts and have law made by interpretation or overturn law made by the people.

This is, of course, a fundamental change in the system devised by our Founding Fathers. Although they created a court system to protect the Constitution, they did not envision the erosion of the legislative process by the court system to the extent it occurs today. But there were fears that the court system with its judges accountable to no one, could become a problem. That is why they set up a system for impeaching federal judges. Impeachment of federal judges rarely happens.

The process makes sense to those who want a change. What would rather do get a law passed in 50 different state legislatures or get a law effectively made in federal courts? Which is the easiest path to take?

But activist judges are not the only change we have made to the justice system. My favorite issue is criminals roaming the streets. Why aren't these people in jail? Not only robbers and burglars but sex offenders! Our children are not safe going to and from school. Indeed, they are not safe in their beds.

Everyday one hears about another child who has been kidnapped and an Amber alert is in process. Many of these children are killed. So not only are they not getting educated, we can't even protect them. What kind of society can't educate and protect its children. Even third world countries can do that.

When I was a kid we left our front door open and did not even lock the screen door. Now I lock all my doors and put a piece of wood in the slot of the sliding doors and windows so they can't be slid open. What a hassle. Every time I go onto the patio I have to stoop over and remove that plank then when I come in I have to put it back. Why? Because we now have "home invasions". In this case, people just come into your house and rob you in your presence. If you resist they will harm you. A man's house is truly his castle these days. I am considering digging a moat.

We were safe in the 50's and before because the justice system worked. I lived in Georgia. If you were convicted of a crime you would find yourself lugging a 50 pound ball around which was attached to your ankle while cutting grass along the roadside and while wearing a black and white stripped uniform. So what happens today? Well, physical labor for prisoners has been eliminated. This work has been contracted out and paid for by the taxpayer – creating jobs. Prison labor is not used. Meanwhile, the prisoners are enjoying prison cells where they have TVs, radios, CD players and Ipods. They also enjoy weight rooms where they can bulk up, basketball courts and softball games. Additional, they have PCs and access to the Internet. Add room and board and free medical care and that is not a bad deal. One prison had a rock band and sold their CDs while their music was being played on MTV!

There is no real punishment these days. "Penitentiary" is derived from the word "penitence". You are supposed to think about your life and where you went wrong. You are supposed to do some introspective thinking. Little of that seems to be going on as is proven by the high recidivism rate.

Add to that that many people found guilty are not even sent to prison. Often there is probation or early release if they happen to go to prison. So how did we go from chain gangs to this?

Also, there is a shortage of prisons. Many prisoners are released early to make room for the incoming prisoners. The Left says that the money that would be used to build more prisons would be better spent in social programs that would prevent crime in the first place. Some say that people commit crime because they are poor. Well that may be but they did have a chance at a free 12 year education after all.

The problem with that thinking is that more prisons work. They keep criminals in jail and thus they keep the streets safe. This way is guaranteed to work. What about more social programs instead? Well, that is not guaranteed to work. After all, we have had many social programs for many years and there is still crime and the streets are still unsafe.

Some see this as merely the cost of doing business. They argue that in a society of 300,000,000 people there is bound to be murders, rapes, robberies and burglaries. Cost of doing business? I am unsafe and have barricade myself in my house and you tell me that this is just the cost of doing business. I find that a lame excuse. Tell the citizens whose children have been raped and murdered that this is the cost of doing business. We simply need to build more prisons. End the early release programs, remove the TVs ad other toys and let these people do penitence. Recidivism rates (number of criminals who re-offend after release from prison) is high. Talks with prison psychologists seem to be doing no good at all. So the only option to reduce crime seems to be put the re-offender back into prison and keep them there this time.

But this is a complicated issue that has economics at its base. The economic model is simple. The more criminals there are on the streets, the more crime there will be. The more crime there is, the more money trial lawyers will make. Remember the Miranda rights quote "if you cannot afford an attorney, one will be appointed for you free of charge." When this went into effect it was sarcastically called the full employment act for lawyers. These lawyers are paid for by the taxpayers. So the trial lawyers benefit economically from this lenient justice system. More crime means more clients. More clients means more money.

The question for the lawyers is how do you keep criminals on the street. Then answer is you get Senators, Congressmen and state legislatures to create a lenient justice system. Now here is the clincher. One of the largest contributors to the Democratic Party is, you guessed it, the Trial Lawyer's Association. That completes the loop. Give money to Democrats to pass lenient laws as regards punishment. This creates more criminals on the street who commit more crime. This creates income for trial lawyers some of which is cycled back to the Democrats for election funds to keep the process going.

So we have a created a flexible legal system replacing the former strict one. Flexibility is a requirement for there to be a "justice industry". Suppose you commit a crime. Further suppose that there is no plea bargaining and there are mandatory sentences. The only thing your lawyer can do is see to it that you get a fair trial in that the prosecution doesn't do anything sneaky like using bad evidence. Now that alone is worth getting a lawyer even though he can't get you off.

But how much more would that lawyer be worth to you if he can get you off? Today they can get you off or at least minimize your punishment. For example, he can use plea bargaining. Plea bargaining is where you agree to plead guilty to a lesser included offense. For example, forcible rape includes assault. So the charge might get plea bargained down from forcible rape to assault. This works for the state since if you plead guilty, no trial is necessary and thus the cost of the trial is eliminated. There is a shortage of prosecutors as there is a shortage of most professionals. Each prosecutor may have dozens of cases he/she is prosecuting. He/she is evaluated based on how fast they dispose of their cases. So he or she is approached by a defense lawyer who is ready to make a deal. "My client", he says, "is charged with driving under the influence of alcohol. He is willing to plead guilty to driving while impaired."

Now the prosecutor has a decision to make. Accepting that plea and the case is over and the prosecutor can add this disposition to his or her weekly progress report. On the other hand if he/she does not accept the plea, then the case goes to court and there is work to do. He/she will accept the plea and move on meanwhile there is now another drunk driver on the road. It may be possible to plea down murder to man slaughter.

A lawyer is worth a lot of money if they can pull things like that off. But this all depends on flexibility in the justice system. If there were no plea bargaining the lawyers would make less money.

Looking at sentencing we see the same thing. To the extent there are mandatory sentences, little can be done to help you. But if the sentencing system in flexible, say, you could get from 5 to 10 years, then something may be done if you get the right lawyer who knows the judge, perhaps they play golf together. Although this is the judge's decision, the point is that the criminal has no knowledge of how to play the game. He needs a lawyer to set this up for him. He might not need the lawyer if there were mandatory sentences because the lawyer could not help him – the sentence is mandatory.

All of this leads to rich lawyers and unsafe streets.

But Democrats have yet another reason to do this. Most crime is committed by the poor. The Democrats represent the poor. So the Clarion call is "put us in office and we will keep your children out of jail." Remember that if you keep the Democrats in power you will also get the activist judges that make law from the bench. These laws always advance the liberal social agenda of the Left. So except for the horrid outcome where the streets are unsafe and you have to blockade yourself in your own home, the system is perfect.

Another change from my time is that lawyers advertise. When I was young I was told that lawyers and doctors do not advertise. These people are professionals and cheap advertising is beneath these professionals. Today we see lawyer advertisements everywhere, on TV, on billboards and in newspapers. It has turned the law from a professional activity into a commercial enterprise. This is an indication of the desperation of an overabundance of lawyers to get work.

Chapter 5

Our Education System

"Education is simply the soul of a society as it passes from one generation to another" - G. K. Chesterton

I feel particularly qualified to write about schools since I was an emergency substitute teacher in my town for 4 years. An emergency substitute is someone who has been certified by the state to teach, but not as a regular teacher. We were called early in the morning when there were not enough regular substitutes available. Regular substitutes are normally certified teachers who do not want to teach full time. Furthermore, many are very particular as to what days they teach, what grades they teach and what schools they teach at. So we emergency substitutes filled in since there has to be an adult with the kids at all times. We have to have a college degree, pass a police background check and supply a lot of references.

Given the doctrine that there has to be an adult with the kids at all times, before this program, the principal might have to take a class. PE might be cancelled for the day and the PE teacher might have to take a class. Front office workers might have to take a class or they may have to close the library and let the librarian teach a class.

The mistake they made by setting up the emergency substitute teacher's program is that it allows ordinary people into the schools. Normally, those in schools are teachers who have been indoctrinated by the teacher's education system. We called them Kool-aid drinkers. They are always ready to defend the current practices in today's schools and always singing the tune that all we need is more money. Thus, with this program, regular people got into the schools and got to see what is going on. I was appalled. The attrition rate from emergency substitute teachers is high as the kids are disrespectful and insubordinate. It is a very stressful if you try to keep order and actually teach. Many don't even try to teach and are just baby sitters.

During those 4 years I learned a lot about our schools. My first day of teaching, and the first time that I had been in secondary schools in 40 years, was horrid. It was 10th grade science. I had to threaten to send one kid to the office if he did not stop playing his guitar. One girl would not get off her cell phone. Everyone was slouching in their seat and it was a great effort just to get them to sit up straight. Many tried to sit on the desk part with their feet in the seat part. It was a horrible experience and I was shocked by the disrespect and insubordination I experienced.

I am not a quitter by nature so I told myself that I would give this a week. But if this is what teaching is like you can count me out. I was an instructor in the Navy and knew how to present material. But the kids would not behave. I could not believe what I was seeing. Fortunately, I have a quick wit. I quickly realized that this was like hecklers in the audience. So I started nailing them. I pointed to one kid who was acting up. I said "class, this is what happens if the mother smokes when she is pregnant". The class roared and the kid, humiliated, sat down and shut up. I told one kid to behave himself. He continued misbehaving. So I said to the class in a most serious and sincere way "does he speak English?" They laughed and he shut up." It turns out that this is a violation of the rules. You can't embarrass or humiliate the student regardless of what they are doing, including disrupting class. It seems that that would affect their self-esteem and these days it's all about the student's self-esteem.

In my day self-esteem came from making good grades but that has all changed. It seems that there has been a revolution in education starting with the Great Society and includes the boomer effect. This revolution required rethinking everything that has been done in schools in 5000 years. Nothing was left unchanged. In fact, the main thing that changed is that the drop out rate has increased and the scores on standard tests have declined when compared to the rest of the world. America's education system, once the best in the world, is in crisis. There are many reasons for this and we will examine some of these changes and their effect on our schools. But it can be shown that this change coincides with boomers becoming teachers. In effect, the 60's revolution continued into the education workplace.

One major change is the "social promotion". It was determined by the socialist Left that being held back to repeat a class was harmful to the self-esteem of the student. It would be better to go ahead and promote the student to the next grade with their peers even if they could not do the work. The so called "social promotion" is now practiced everywhere. Few kids get held back anymore. For my generation the threat of getting held back was motivation to study. That motivation is now gone.

But there is a more insidious reason for the social promotion. First, to hold a kid back is sure to start a war with the kid's parents. Parents these days always take the kid's side when dealing with schools. It's the way they show the kid that they love them. The charge will be made that it is the teacher who has failed to teach rather than the student who has failed to learn. The parents will appeal to the principal and even the school superintendent, perhaps even the school board. If you were a teacher you would find it easier to just promote the kid and be done with it. After all, if all your kids get promoted to the next grade, then you must be a good teacher.

Next came grade inflation. If a kid gets Fs on everything then how can you possibly promote them to the next grade?

The solution to that dilemma is simple – just give them Cs and Ds on everything. If fact, you will look like a good teacher if all your kids get As and Bs so just give all of them good grades. This is called "grade inflation" and it's happening. The way to accomplish this is to make the tests easy. Rather than converting 17/31 to a decimal make the question convert 1/4 to a decimal. Easy tests and high scores. Then when there are standard tests with more difficult questions, the kids do poorly.

In my state 50% of the 10th graders can not pass the state's standard math test which is actually 8th grade math. Yet 100% of the kids pass math class and get promoted. Hmmmm.

I once saw a girl on TV who was devastated. It seems that she had made As and Bs all through school in math. When she got to college, she was put in remedial math. Grade inflation is real.

So schools have become a pipe line through which all kids move with social promotion and come out the other end with fairly good grades thanks to grade inflation. Only standard tests can show what is really going on. The SAT scores began to fall. Since these numbers represent averages of all students across the nation, these numbers are statistically valid. When these numbers show that minorities did worse than non-minorities, the charge was quickly made that the test was racially biased. Only white kids can pass these tests because of the nature of the questions. It's hard to imagine a racially biased math test. Perhaps History and English Literature but Math?

The No Child Left Behind (NCLB) Act was an attempt to fix our schools. It called for each state to set up standardized tests for evaluating their schools. But the immediate reaction from parents and teachers was to claim that these tests were poorly constructed and racially biased. NCLB is currently up for renewal. The powerful teachers unions in Washington D.C.

are fighting it already, calling for more "reasonable" tests. If you can read between the lines, this translates to easier tests. The kids have all heard of NCLB and from its name, they may form the opinion that they will get promoted regardless of their level of work. The name does imply that. Perhaps we should call it the SGLB test - Study or Get Left Behind.

The theory was that the schools work but the standard tests do not show what the kids know. What a convenient theory if you are in the school business. So many colleges have stopped using the SAT as a requirement for admission. Nor do they have their own test. They just accept the grade point average of a student but recall that we have grade inflation.

I don't have a particular problem with this college admission criteria. In fact, I would say let everybody have a chance at one quarter of college. If they get Cs they can stay in. But that would soon lead to a system where everybody got Cs. Colleges are businesses and students are customers. Businesses want as many customers as they can get. The theory seems to be "if you have the tuition then we have the classroom seat."

One of the changes that has taken place is the way we teach Math. It began as the "New Math". Everybody remembers when the parents could not help their kids with their homework. That has been dropped and it has been admitted that that did not work but not before an entire generation of kids was produced that cannot do simple Math like arithmetic.

But the New Math was replaced by more methodologies to teach math. All of this is based on the belief that schooling should be more than mere memorization. The problem with that thinking is that the multiplication, addition and subtraction tables have to be memorized. There is no other way apart from counting on your fingers. When you ask someone what 3 plus 4 is and they start counting on their fingers, they look stupid.

There is a doctrine in academia called "publish or perish. That means that PhDs must do more than just teach a couple of classes each day. They must write books and articles. The motivation for this is that universities measure themselves on how many books and articles that their professors have written. The more books their professors have written, the higher the tuition can be because the university has famous professors.

Now suppose you are a professor in the Education department. What you need to do is to come up with a new methodology to teach, say, Math. This is where all these new methodologies come from. Beyond that, it would be nice to have it adopted by, say, the National Association of Mathematics Teachers. Next it is in schools. Adopting new methodologies for teaching math, English and even Science is the way that school boards and state education agencies make it look like the schools are being improved and by extension, that they are doing their jobs. So we are paraded by a train of new methodologies for teaching. Also, those who print text books are always ready to sell new books to replace existing books. The problem with this, especially with Math, is that there was nothing wrong with the way it was done in the 50's. We all learned to do arithmetic with fractions, decimals and make the necessary conversions.

But that required memorizing the multiplication tables and the algorithms for this arithmetic. When you buy into the idea that school should be more than memorizing, then you buy into dropping the way that worked for centuries and substituting these methodologies – New Math, Reform Math, Discovery Math, Constructionist Math California Math and Integrated Math, to name a few Math teaching methodologies. The problem with these methodologies is that kids can't do math these days. Think I'm crazy, think I'm exaggerating? Ask a kid you know above the 5th grade to convert this to a decimal.

1/7 + 6.126/.056 - .32 x .83 – 1/3

See if the kid can do this simple arithmetic problem. To make it harder, ask him/her to carry the answer out to 5 decimal digits. Few kids today can do this. Today and especially in the future, few adults will be able to solve this problem.

Kid's math skills today are pathetic. Ask a kid you know to add 5/6 and 1/4 and again see for yourself. Ask them to find 17% of $35. Ask them to divide 13547 by 167 and carry the answer out to 5 decimal places.

If kids can't do arithmetic then they can't do Algebra or the calculations required in Science class. So they fail at Algebra and Science as well.

Still another change in the education system from say, the 50's, is the basic relationship between the teacher and the student. In the 50's the teacher was an authority figure. The teacher presented material, the student learned it and there was a test to see how well the student learned it. It was a simple process and those who misbehaved were sent to the principal's office.

Then a theory came along that said that the teacher should be the student's friend. It started with discipline problems. The thought was that the student would behave if the teacher was their friend. In theory it should not matter. So teachers made special efforts to have a personal relationship with their students. Notice that is does not happen in college. This may or may not work but it shouldn't be necessary. The kids should behave or be sent to the office and their parents called to let them know that their child has been kicked out of class for misbehaving. Then the parents should take away the kid's cell phone and Ipod. But this is far too drastic for liberal thinkers. Thus, many schools have hired psychologists to have a touchy-feely talk with the misbehaving student. This is not discipline.

And the folks in the office claim that they are busy and do not have time to deal with discipline problems. Most principals tell the teachers that he/she expects the teacher to take care of their discipline problems and not to send kids to the office. If I were a principal I would say the exact opposite. I would say "Don't take time away from your teaching to deal with discipline problems. If you have any ongoing problems with a kid, just send them to the office and I will take care of it. You teach."

But that is not how the system works. This did not really come up in the 50's because the kids behaved. I was sent to the principal's office on occasion. I once, as a substitute, sent a kid to the office and they sent him right back. He walked back into class like the winner of our dispute. He was a hero to the other kids. I was appalled.

Yet we are putting more money into education than at any time in history. So what isn't working? All we hear is that schools need more money. If we had more money to pay teachers then we would have better teachers. That very statement has a problem since it implies that after all the education, after the rigorous teacher certification process which includes practice teaching, many teachers can't teach. Before we go any further with this, we should ask what is wrong with the education and certification process now in place? Maybe that is what has to be fixed. It is apparently producing teachers who can't teach.

But there is a bigger problem with this approach of more money produces better teachers. First, if we even doubled the teacher's salaries, it would take at least 20 years to replace all the current teachers through retirement and attrition. Can we wait for 20 years? What would happen is that the current teachers would get a big pay increase. Would this increase in pay make them better teachers? If you say yes then you are saying that today's teachers are holding back and not teaching as well as they could and that they would give it their all if they were making more money.

Is that what is happening? I doubt that the teacher's union would agree with that. We can presume that they are doing their inadequate best. So how about this? New teachers coming into teaching get higher pay than those already teaching. This will attract better teachers. Well what do you think the teacher's union will have to say about that idea?

So the real problem seems to be the teacher's unions. The unions protect weak teachers. It's almost impossible to fire a teacher. Union contracts say that they be put on probation and observed with the observations documented. That's a lot of work. Then they should be sent for more training, while drawing their full salary of course. But wait. Didn't they get a degree from college in education and pass a rigorous certification process? The unions fight any changes to reform education. They fight any efforts to evaluate teachers for performance. Teachers are the only workers in the American economy who are not evaluated. Few are fired despite the dismal performance of schools.

I am currently trying to get our school board to establish the following policies.

Policy 1. It will be the policy of the school district to use the police department's drug sniffing dog to randomly sniff lockers at middle schools and high schools which have lockers. This sniffing will include gym lockers. The school district will enter into an agreement with the police department to arrange for scheduling. It has been previously determined that there is no cost required for this. This is legal and has been tested in the courts.

Policy 2. It will be the policy of the school district that teachers will dress as professionals when teaching class. For men this will require a dress shirt and tie. For women this will include dresses or pants suits. Forbidden will be blue jeans, T shirts and sneakers.

Policy 3. It will be the policy of the school district that teachers will not cover up the window of their classroom door to the hall. This will allow the principal to view the conduct of students and the teacher in the classroom if the door is closed.

Policy 4. It will be the policy of the school district that principals will patrol the halls several times each day to look for infractions of school policies. Students in violation will be taken to the office and their parents will be called.

Policy 5. It will be the policy of the school district that students will not use their cell phones and/or music devices during class or during change time. Cell phones may be used anytime there is an emergency.

Policy 6. It will be the policy of the school district that tests which will have an impact on grades will be taken home, signed by the parent(s) and returned to the teacher the next day to engage the parents in their child's education.

Policy 7. It will be the policy of the school district that pictures and posters hung in the classroom on a permanent basis must have something to do with education. Forbidden are pictures and posters of movie stars, sports figures, popular contemporary musicians and singers. Acceptable are maps, the multiplication tables, the periodic table, pictures of historically famous people, geometric shapes, the solar system, famous quotations, and the like.

I am meeting great resistance to establishing these common sense policies. Our school board will not even allow these things to be discussed in public at school board meetings.

They claim that they are discussing these things in their work study meetings. They refuse to put these things on the agenda for public discussion.

The teacher's union seems to feel that they have to nip in the bud, any changes to the way they have things set up. Otherwise, there may be a plethora of changes coming down the pike. These ideas have to be stopped in their tracks is the thinking.

Our school board President said in the newspaper that requiring professional dress for teachers would be a change in "working conditions" and would require union approval in accordance with the wording of their contract. Fine, I say. So let's force the issue and force the union to take the public position that they do not want to wear professional dress to school while at the same time calling themselves professionals and insisting on being paid as professionals. Let's let the pubic hear that.

But our school board members, like most school board members, are not exactly profiles in courage. All they seem to want is peace in the family and not to rock the boat and ruffle any feathers, especially the feathers of the powerful teacher's union.

So it's hard to believe that more money is the answer to our woes. This solution is popular because governments cannot envision a solution to any problem if more money is not the solution. If more money can't fix it, then it can't be fixed is their thinking.

Colleges have long felt that they are apart from society in general. They have their own campus police and feel that there is no room for government interference. Lower schools are starting to adopt this attitude. Using the excuse of sexual predators, the public and press are kept out of schools, the schools they pay for with their tax dollars. You have to check in at the desk, which is OK, then you are asked what you want. Just say I want to look around and see what is going on in the classes. Lots of luck.

Now we are being told that all this is the parents fault. The latest theory is that the parents do not motivate their children to learn. Yet we hear that teachers do more than teach. This is their defense when it is suggested that teachers be evaluated with tests. They are on record as saying that tests do not test what you know. When this happens the teachers say that teachers do more than teach. They motivate and inspire students which can't be tested for. Well, that's all well and good but it does not fit with the notion that the parents are not motivating their children. It sounds like here that the teachers are supposed to be doing the motivating. This is why we can't evaluate them on merely how well they teach.

I think that it is possible to teach kids that are in orphanages and who don't even have any parents.

Also, we are told that the parents do not help their kids with their homework. One parent told me this. "They have my kid for 6 hours a day. Isn't that enough time to teach my kid fractions? Now I am being asked to teach them fractions at home." That is a valid point so why are we blaming the parents? Well the answer to that is simple. If we don't blame the parents then we have to blame the schools and the teachers. The teachers have a union but the parents do not.

It may well be the parent's fault to some extent. They should motivate their kids to study and to go on to college or trade school for example. So a compromise is forming. We now hear that the education of children requires a partnership between teachers and parents. Parents who fall for this are simply enjoining themselves in the problem and setting themselves up for sharing in the blame.

I happen to believe that the schools have the kids for enough time to educate the children even if there were no homework at all. But I do believe in homework because we learn through practice. Practice, practice, practice is how we learn arithmetic and the multiplication tables. Homework provides an opportunity for practice. But even without homework it should be possible to teach these things to kids having them for 6 hours a day.

I decided to look at a typical teaching day in our district. Let me warn you that these numbers may vary from district to district and state to state.

As a substitute teacher, I was amazed to find how easy it was to teach elementary school. In high school teachers teach 5 periods of different students with 30 minutes for lunch. That makes for a long day especially when you add in the discipline issues. Here is the breakdown of a typical elementary school teacher's day in my district. Every time I turned around I was on a break. (This will vary slightly from school to school, that is, some schools may get only 45 minutes for lunch and some schools may have only 25 minutes for recesses. But in general the following is true.)

First, teachers work a 7 1/2 hour day. So how much of that time are they actually delivering educational material – "teaching" as the word is used herein? Well, they are required to be there 30 minutes before school starts and stay there for 30 minutes after school ends. The kids are not there. So that's 6 1/2 half hours of possible teaching. But the children get a 30 minute recess in the morning and in the afternoon. So that's 5

1/2 hours of possible teaching. But there is a one hour lunch break where the children get another recess after eating. So that's 4 1/2 hours of possible teaching. But the children take a 30 minute class in music, PE or the library each day so that leaves 4 hours of possible teaching. Then our district emphasizes reading so the children do 30 minutes of silent reading each day. (The teacher is there but not teaching). So now we are down to 3 1/2 hours of possible teaching each day. I take away another 15 minutes in the morning when the children are putting away their back packs and sitting down, getting organized, the teacher is taking attendance, doing the lunch count, collecting homework, listening to the morning announcements, saying the Pledge of Allegiance and 15 minutes in the afternoon when the children are cleaning up the classroom, collecting their books and papers, putting on their jackets and back packs before being dismissed. Now we are down to 3 hours. Add to this the 5 minutes here and there when the kids are getting in line to go to recess, music, PE or library, and lunch and being marched to their destination by the teacher. It adds up to at least 15 minutes a day. So now we are down to 2 hours and 45 minutes of possible actual teaching time – delivering material.

Imagine that. Out of a 7 1/2 half hour day, the teacher is actually delivering material to the students for less than 3 hours. What is wrong with this picture? Actual teaching (delivery of information) has become a part time job. Then they get all national holidays off plus a few personal holidays plus a long Thanksgiving, Christmas, and Spring break and they are off for three months in the summer while receiving a nice salary and healthcare and retirement benefits, sick leave and wear casual dress to work with little or no supervision and expected to work independently. It's hard to imagine a better job than that.

Now I wish to point out that teachers do work all day long. Even getting kids organized in the morning is work. Then there are papers to grade and work sheets to make up, but they do have nearly 5 hours a day for this by the above numbers. I am talking about the delivery of information. Check with your kids and do the math for yourself. In that 2 hours and 45 minutes each day they have to teach English, Arithmetic, Spelling, Social Studies (includes History and Geography), and Art. That is about 30 minutes a day for each subject.

This bodes well for home schooling. If there is only 2 hours and 45 minutes of actual delivery of material each day, then parents can easily do that in the evenings. Many parents are doing just that. Having lost faith in the schools and not wanting their kids subjected to today's school environment, which now includes drugs, they keep their kids at home and home school them. There are many websites that offer lessons and tests for this.

But this assumes that at least one parent does not work and stays at home. In today's economy, unlike the economy of the 50's, both parents usually work. School then becomes daycare for their kids. The strictest rule I found when I was teaching was that there had to be an adult with the kids at all times. This too is a change from when I went to school. I clearly remember the teacher leaving the class room to go to the office or to go to mimeograph a test or work sheet. We sat there and did our work knowing that if she walked in and caught us misbehaving we would be in big trouble. This might include no recess for a few days. But today's teachers do not like to withhold recess as punishment. Why? Because during recess the teacher gets a 30 minute break. If you withhold recess, you lose the 30 minute break. I was surprised that our teachers send kids on recess when it is cold and even when it is raining or at least drizzling. I have seen kids in recess standing up against the building and under the eve of the roof so as not to get wet while the teacher is on a 30 minute break.

Getting held after school is out as punishment also since

nearly all the kids now ride the bus to school. They can't be held after school since they will miss their bus.

Since there are now many options to public school, parents with a significant amount of money use them. There are parochial schools, private schools and now charter schools as options. This of course creates a two tier school system, one for the rich and one for the poor. Later, this will create a rigid class system with the kids of the rich running things while the kids of the poor will not be able to add two fractions together.

This trend of a two tier education system will have political ramifications in the future. Now we can tell the losers in society that their lot in life is their own fault. We can say that you went to the same schools and had the same teachers as everyone else. They succeeded and you failed.

But in the future that will not be true. They will argue that they went to public schools while the successful citizens went to parochial, private or charter schools. They will argue that they did not get a good education and as a result, they are poor. They will argue that they never had a chance. And they will be right.

So are we stuck with this situation? Well in theory we can fix our schools but in practice we cannot. The problem is the teacher's unions and the bureaucrats in the school districts. Let's start with the bureaucrats first. Bureaucrats are, by their very nature, delegators. They want to keep the work day easy. So they delegate things down to the principal at the individual schools. Each school becomes a self-contained unit. Principals, at least in my district, set policies for everything in their schools.

This, of course, results in every school being different which results in good schools and bad schools, depending on whether or not they have a good principal or a bad principal.

The thinking amongst the bureaucrats is that the principal, teachers and parents through their PTA can run the school as they see fit. This is the doctrine of local control of schools carried to the extreme. Any problem at the school is answered by "you have total control so it's your fault." That lets the highly paid bureaucrats off the hook.

But it gets worse from there. Most principals, if they have any effective policies at all, leave everything up to the teacher through more delegation. Thus, each classroom becomes a self-contained unit. Teachers are free to decorate their classroom any way they like claiming that this is their office. I once taught in a classroom that had pictures of basketball players hung everywhere because the teacher was a basketball fan. I taught in a classroom where there were sofas and arm chairs everywhere instead of desks. It was like being in someone's living room, complete with lamps instead of the overhead lights which were turned off. Throw rugs on the floor completed the informal environment.

Then teachers are free to seat the kids anyway they like. In the 50's we sat in rows and there was a sense of individuality. Now the kids are organized into pods, 4 kids to a pod. These are little teams and not individuals. Usually the smartest kid in the pod does the works and the other kids copy it. With the pod arrangement one kid at the pod has his back to the front of the room and thus to the teacher if the teacher is standing at the front of the room.

I once was having a terrible time with a 4th grade class. When they went to recess I rearranged their seats into rows. Returning they were shocked. They were all forced to look to the front where I was standing. I had no more trouble with them since I had thrown them off balance. Eliminating their social pods, they were individuals.

Other seating arrangements I observed were to have the kids sit in a circle or semi-circle. I rarely saw rows like we experienced in the 50's. But it seems that it could be argued that there is a best way to seat kids to achieve the best learning environment. Once that is identified, then all classrooms should be organized that way. Seems like a good idea so what is the problem? The problem is the teacher's unions who would fight any such proposal as they fight any proposal to evaluate teachers for effectiveness.

So although it is theoretically possible to fix our schools, it is not practically possible because of the powerful teacher's unions. Thus the two tier school system is our only choice.

Yet another change in schools is the relationship between the kids themselves. In my day the smart kids were admired. The goal was to have smart kids. Today, the smart kids are called geeks and nerds. The goal is to focus on the majority of kids which are the average kids. I appreciate addressing the needs of all the kids but the thinking seems to be that the smart kids can take care of themselves. Fortunately, most schools have advanced classes where the smart kids can reach their full potential. Some argue that this is discrimination against the poor.

The most alarming thing about today's schools is the fat child epidemic. This is not entirely the school's fault but they do play a role. The fat child epidemic is worrisome because it has been predicted that many of these kids will have diabetes when they grow up and more health problems in general. Obesity is a direct cause of many illnesses like heart disease. So what role do the schools play?

Well first it's the lunches the kids are served. When I began teaching, I would buy the student lunch. I quickly ended that practice. There is pizza served at least once a week. Pizza, at its best, contains a lot of fat but this pizza was little more than doughy bread, topped with spicy ketchup and loaded with cheese. Then there were hot dogs and you can bet that they were not all beef probably not even all meat. Then fried chicken. Nearly everything was fried since the central kitchen has to prepare thousands of meals a day and frying is the fastest way to do that. To the school's credit, each kid gets a piece of fruit and a cartoon of milk each day, but a small carton and only one carton even if they ask for another. I would say give them all the milk they are willing to drink and all the fruit they are willing to eat.

In high schools there is a deli where one can get a healthy turkey sandwich but there is also a pizza stand where one can get a greasy pizza. Most students choose the pizza.

Then there are the vending machines in middle and high schools. Rows of them selling soft drinks and candy bars. The kids just fill up on sugar and many get fat. At school we have an opportunity to give every kid in America at least one healthy meal each day but we do not do that.

Fast food restaurants are trying to get into schools to sell their unhealthy meals there. The schools need the money which is why the vending machines are in the schools in the first place so we can be sure that the hamburger joints are soon to follow.

Finally, there are the toys used to teach kids. The idea is to make learning fun. Well learning is work and should be seen as work. This is OK for kids under 5 but school should be seen as a serious place. We do not need Mickey Mouse teaching the kids the multiplication tables. We need teachers teaching the kids the multiplication tables. There is a danger of kids learning everything through computer games and other software. There is a place for this software but it's not to replace the teacher.

Chapter 6

The 5th Estate

"All the news that's fit to print." - slogan of the New York Times

The 5th estate is a term that now refers to the press. The 4th estate originally referred to the press and has it's origins in the French Revolution. In May 1789, Louis XVI summoned to Versailles a full meeting of the Estates General. The First Estate consisted of three hundred nobles. The Second Estate, three hundred clergy. The Third Estate, six hundred commoners. Some years later, after the French Revolution, Edmund Burke, looking up at the Press Gallery of the House of Commons, said, 'Yonder sits the Fourth Estate, and they are more important than them all."

The 5th esate is based on the understanding that, over the last 50 years, the mass media have systematically failed to act as the critical 4th Estate that they have pretended to be. Instead, they have consistently represented the interests of, and functioned as an integral component of the elites controlling society and determining policy. These are, in fact, the Liberals.

The press has a critical role to play in Democracy. They are the providers of the information that the public uses to decide on whom to vote for. Thus, the press is supposed to be objective. Bias in the press goes back to the very beginning of our government. Both parties had their own newspapers during the early elections. What was supposed to make this work was that there would be several papers to choose from. Get the ideas and opinions of all papers and then make up your own mind.

Indeed, most large cities had several papers, typically one liberal and one conservative. But over time more and more cities became one newspaper towns, at least there is only one major paper. This is true today. So is that paper liberal or conservative?

Papers are businesses who derive their income, not from the sale of papers but from advertising. But high revenue advertising is possible only if the paper has a large circulation. So how do you get people to subscribe to your paper? Well, certainly not by printing things that they object to reading. So papers, as well as radio and TV have to appeal to their audiences as well as try to be objective in their presentations of the news, the facts. This is often difficult to do and if a choice has to be made, it's better to come down on the side of your reader's desires.

If you look at the famous map of red and blue states you see a lot of blue states, especially along both coasts. But if you look at this map at the county level, the first division of states is counties, then you will see that many blue states are mostly red when seen at the county level. Indeed, the blue part of blue states are the major cities in the state. It's easy to explain this. Blue represents liberalism and red represents conservatism. Liberals address social issues providing aid to those in need. So where are those in need located? The big cities. Big cities are where the homeless are. Big cities are where the unemployment is. Big cities are where the crime is. Big cities are where the poor are. So big cities are where the Liberals are. Big cities are typically liberal in their political thinking. People in big cities need government involvement in their lives. Rural farmers and small cities typically do not and so tend to be conservative. These people are generally more self-sufficient.

Now suppose you publish a paper in a big city. What slant should you put on the news to make your paper appeal to your readers? The Leftist slant of course. Therefore, more big city papers are liberal in their political thinking and write stories in such a way that they appeal to their liberal readers. Remember that newspapers and Radio & TV stations are businesses trying to make money. Their readers are their customers. They give their customers what they want in the same way that all businesses give their customers what they want.

Liberals want to hear that the Afghanistan war is going bad. This will increase the chances of a president from the Democratic Party. So big city papers print stories that the war is going bad and their readers like to read that. It's easy to do. There are some good things happening in the war and some bad things. You have only so much space for the story so you only print the bad things.

What is supposed to happen is that the other major paper in the city might print the other side of the story. But most big cities only have one major paper. Even where there are two papers they are often owned by the same company and have the same editorial board.

Now there are big cities that have conservative papers. And predictably these cities are in red states and red counties where there is already a conservative readership. So most papers are not enlightening people, most papers and radio & TV stations are, as we say, preaching to the choir. They are merely affirming what the readership already thinks. In that sense they are playing a harmful role by curtailing objective, independent thinking among their readers. They are reinforcing what may be an erroneous position in public thinking. This might cause people to miscast their vote in the election.

So more than a vast left-wing conspiracy to take over the press, it's more a group of businessmen trying to make a profit by appealing to their customers and thus writing what their customers want to read. The problem is the lack of competition. But that is explainable as well. Suppose you are a conservative media outlet in a liberal big city. How many customers are you going to have? Not enough to stay in business.

Local papers were once the only source of news for the public. But that has been changed by technology. We now have radio and TV and now even blogs on the Internet. There is now national news presented nationally. So now the question becomes how should they slant the news. America is currently split about 50/50 between Liberals and Conservatives. Most national TV media tends to present the liberal view but there are cable channels like Fox news which claim to be fair and balanced. None of the national TV news programs even claim this, they just don't bring it up. With the county split 50/50 you might flip a coin to get your slant but recall that most of the Liberals are in the big cities and most of the Conservatives are in small towns and in the country side.

Now it becomes an issue of which group watches TV the most and, more importantly, which group might be motivated by a commercial to go out and buy the product being advertised. That is probably the group in the big cities. Shopping and spending money in the big cities is a sport. People in the country, being more conservative with their spending, tend to buy only what they need. People in the big cities, in the race to keep up with the Jones, tend to buy what they want even though they may not actually need it.

So rather than flip a coin to get your slant, apply these principles and slant the news towards those in the big cities, that is, employ the liberal slant. Again, liberalism in national TV news is not a conspiracy, its just good business.

But the point is that the news is slanted and it's slanted towards the Left. Thus voters often make their decision based on this leftist slant of the news.

Chapter 7

The Boomer Effect

"The young always have the same problem - how to rebel and conform at the same time. They have now solved this problem by defying their parents and copying one another"- Quentin Crisp

Nothing has had a greater effect on America in the last half century than the boomer generation. All generations have an effect on their country but none to this degree.

Who are the boomers? Well they have gone by various names, like baby boomers or just boomers and some are called hippies and yuppies, but boomer seems to have lasted the longest. Basically, they were the children who were born in the years immediately after World War II ended. The war ended in 1946 and millions of soldiers came home. Naturally, these soldiers got married and began having children. This produced a boom in child births called the baby boom. Many of them went on to become yuppies, an acronym for Young Upwardly Mobil Professionals (YUPPIES).

Their upbringing was guided by a famous book written by Dr. Jonas Spock, "Baby and Childcare". He had a theory on how to raise kids and many people followed it. It was a departure from traditional child rearing techniques and said among other thing that you should not spank your child. He was in disagreement with the Bible which says "spare the rod and spoil the child." Before he died, he publicly recanted his theories but not before creating the boomer generation. Thus, the rod was spared and we got what some call the spoiled brats of the American Empire.

Their effect began as soon as they reached school age. There were not enough schools to take care of this influx of children so a massive school building program was begun. It is felt by some that by their sheer numbers they became a social unit unto themselves and apart from the general American Society. I once had a boomer friend boast that by our sheer numbers, we will always get what we want. He turned out to be right. This is because President Lyndon got the Constitution amended and gave them the vote. He felt that they would be young idealists and have liberal attitudes and vote for the Democrats. As a separate social unit they developed their own values, rejecting the values of their parents. They had their own culture. This caused a break to occur in the values that had been handed down from generation to generation. This break continues to this day. In that sense we are producing generation after generation of kids who are not inheriting the value system that had been handed down from prior generations. These kids are, in fact, lost generations, like ships without a rudder.

Some of the values they are missing are, for example, personal responsibility, being responsible for your own actions. Psychologist and sociologists are working overtime thinking up excuses for kids these days. Perhaps they come from bad homes or perhaps they come from single parent families. Perhaps everyone is doing this so that it is in fact normal. Perhaps it is the shows that they see on TV (which are protected by the First Amendment by the way). Perhaps it's ADD. Some say let them be kids and enjoy their childhood. These messages filter down to the kids who readily accept them.

Another value is the hard work ethic. My generation got allowances and only when we cut the grass and did other chores. Today's kids benefit from a plethora of gifts like cell phones, Ipods, Xboxes and the like. Do they have to make good grades to earn these gifts? Well the national scholastics scores do not bear this out. This can clearly be traced to the boomer generation who were the most fortunate generation in history in that regard. The boomers had everything as their parents enjoyed the fruits of our victory in WWII. We became the richest nation in the world and the boomer kids became the richest children in the world. Kids today do not have the sense that they must work for what they get. It just comes to them for the asking, often from parents who cannot give them quality time.

So for a start we have kids who have little sense of personal responsibility and get nearly everything they ask for.

Respect for authority is another missing value. Kids never say "yes sir" and "yes ma'am" anymore, not to their teachers nor to their parents. We were taught to show respect to any adult. I said "yes sir" and "yes ma'am" to all the adults who lived on my block and, of course to my teachers.

This is not a trivial matter since schools are supposed to be training future adults and in the adult world there are many people who you will have to show respect for like your boss and particularly his boss. This too can be traced to the boomer generation whose motto was "never trust anybody over 30." This ties directly to obedience which today's kids are not good at. The boomers were disobedient with little respect for the law. They had rallies where many girls went topless. They smoked marijuana and used other drugs. The boomers are directly responsible for America's drug problem today. They flaunted authority wherever they found it. Today's kids have inherited this behavior.

Their next major impact was when they entered college. They changed the college experience completely. There was free love and the drug culture was born. Their dress was atrocious by previous standards. Some were called hippies. They marched. They took over the administration buildings, protested the war and generally tried to change everything and they were very proud of this. They saw themselves as romantic revolutionaries, over turning a system that did not work and replacing it with a system that was based on love and the idea of doing your own thing – a system based on freedom. They were responsible for the success of the Beatles and the British invasion in general as our music culture changed drastically. The 60's was a romantic era.

Then they were known as boomers and every thing was about love and peace. This is because they had not yet discovered Rolex watches and BMWs. When they finished school they entered the workplace, they discovered these things, life's material things. Having little morals in the traditional sense, because they had rejected the values of the past, they were easily manipulated. Anything the boss wanted was OK by them. They were more than happy to help whatever the company was doing be it legal or illegal as long as they were getting ahead.

As they began making money they did discover Rolex watches and BMWs. The main thing about them was their lack of individualism. What one wore, they all wore. What one drove, they all drove. What one listened to in music, they all listened to. They were all like carbon copies of each other, all cut from the same mold. But there was so many of them, boomers everywhere. And they were a self-contained social unit.

They became known as the "me" generation. They were proud to be known as the selfish sounding "me" generation. They were selfish and very competitive. One can detail the changes as they moved through the workplace. They became middle managers, then Vice Presidents. Today they are chief executives who brought us the recent economic collapse. Next they will bankrupt Social Security and Medicare.

Their children are now on the scene. These kids are called "reverbs." (from the noun reverberation which is a form of echo.) The reverbs are in their 20's and 30's. The boomers are the grandparents of today's children.

Today we see TV commercials about staying young, working out, jogging, losing weight, etc. These are all being addressed to the aging boomers. Soon, as they continue to age, we will be flooded with commercials about hearing aids, walkers, and the things that old people need.

But such is life. Today college campuses have been yuppified as well as society in general.

Most of the changes outlined in this book are a direct result of the boomers. They changed the culture and the following generation, called the X generation, are carrying this on. But the X generation tended to reject much of the boomer philosophy. In general, the X generation does not like the boomers thinking, seeming to them to be too materialistic. Many X generation members have dropped out of the material society created by the boomers. This is to their credit but a bit of an over reaction. For example, the boomers did not pierce their bodies and get tattooed. They did not dye their hair orange or purple. They did not wear leather with spikes. This is all X generation behavior but was created by the freedom which boomers put in place or at least reaction to the boomers.

The biggest thing that the boomer generation represents is a complete disconnect with what has gone before. Normally, culture is handed down from one generation to another with slight changes along they way. This continuity was totally disrupted by the boomer generation. They rejected every thing that had gone before. When they were in their twenties the watch word was "never trust anyone over 30. When they entered their 30's that philosophy changed.

One thing that was consistent with the boomers was the immediacy of their philosophy of life. Everything was about what works right now with no thought on how this might play out in the future. It was all "me" and "now".

The parents of the boomers are known as "the greatest generation". This was the generation that won World War II and saved the world from the Fascists. They do deserve that credit but on the other side of the ledger they did produce the boomer generation which has had a great negative effect on the American society. The drug problem is rampant today because of the boomers. AIDS and other sexually transmitted diseases are rampant because of the boomer's casual attitude towards sex in the sixties. Pornography today is also a result of this. Make no mistake they changed America.

One can ask how did the greatest generation could produce a generation like this? The greatest generation had suffered war. This usually makes people wise and possibly good parents later. Their parents were, however, very materialistic themselves. They got to enjoy the fruits of the war as America became the richest nation that had ever existed in history. And the greatest generation indulged to excess. They felt that this was their reward for winning the war.

Again, for the record, Dr. Spock has admitted publicly that he was wrong in his theory on raising children. But he has recanted too late. The damage has been done. The question is how good are the boomers as parents. Their children are entering their 20's and 30's. Perhaps they will see their grandchildren using drugs in the culture that they themselves created. As we say "what goes around, comes around."

Bill Clinton was the first boomer President. It was inevitable that there would be a boomer President one day. A typical boomer lacking in morals he had had affairs but this is not immoral behavior to boomers. After all, they liberated sex.

Sex for them required no emotional relationship. You just do it, what is the big deal? With that attitude what you are doing is not immoral. What is all the fuss about?

When it came to the Monica Lewenski affair he seriously could not understand what this was about. What did I do wrong was his thinking. It was just oral sex, no big deal. This must be the vast right wing conspiracy at work.

His conduct throughout was appalling. Getting his cabinet to lie for him. Lying himself to the American people.

In Bartlett's Famous Quotations his memorable line will be "It depends on what the meaning of "is" is." This is a combination of two of the worse possible things - a lawyer talking and a boomer talking. What the meaning of "is" is? What an absurd position to take. We all know what "is" means. It showed a certain boomer arrogance. To be fair, the FBI did not ask the question correctly. They asked "is there a relationship between you and Ms. Lewenski?" They should have asked "is there or has there ever been a relationship between you and Ms. Lewenski." It is possible that the question was rigged just to allow President Clinton to dance his way out of the answer later if necessary. I say this because it is such an obvious mistake to ask the question in the way they did. These are government lawyers after all who are doing the asking and they did work for President Clinton.

So the first boomer President goes down in history as a President that was impeached (but not convicted).

Our 2nd boomer President was George W. Bush. His problem is that he is a CEO by training and runs cabinet meetings like staff meetings. Unfortunately, Bush has no vision. Visions require a moral foundation that the boomers lack. When Reagan, who had a vision, held a meeting he gave orders as to what he wanted done. When Bush held a meeting he asked for advice as to what to do. That's all you can do if you have no vision. He then probably goes with the majority ignoring the advice of the one genius in the room. That is what CEOs do.

This lack of vision comes from the fact, as I said above, that boomers lived with a "me/now" attitude. They were given anything they wanted and enjoyed the fruits of the American Empire that their fathers had produced by winning the war. The generation can be characterized by the catch phrase of the time – "sex, drugs and rock and roll".

How long will this run of boomer Presidents last? Well despite the behavior of Bill Clinton he is the most liked man in the Democratic Party. And then his wife Hillary, a boomer herself, had her eyes set on that office and expected it to be a positive that she is the wife of Bill Clinton. Imagine if you will this scenario. She became President and got Bill made head of the United Nations. These two boomers would have run planet Earth. There is never a Martian invasion around when you need one.

Most of the other Presidential candidates are boomers. If they are no better than the last two, then a curious trick of history will occur. The children of the greatest generation that created the American Empire will destroy it. Historians will have a field day with that one.

What has happened to America is not an unusual occurrence in history. The real men, hardened by life, wise from experience and bold by nature create an empire or kingdom and their children, spoiled by riches, naive by protection from harsh reality, lose the kingdom. So we are right on track in that regard.

In summary, the boomers, emboldened by their sheer numbers rejected the values of the past and created their own value system based on me/now and do your own thing. Each forthcoming generation continues this process of establishing a value system that is convenient to their thinking at the time and rejecting a value system that is inconvenient to their thinking. Some Liberals actually think of this as freedom, where values, and the restrictions they impose, limit individual freedoms.

Today, in many states, pregnant young girls are free to get an abortion without their parents even knowing about it. Is it any of the parents business? Of course it is and here is why. The girl was obviously having sex without protection. We know that because that is how she got pregnant. Well, luckily, she only got pregnant. She could have acquired the HIV virus by having unprotected sex. Now if that happened would that be the business of the parents? You bet. This would have made it difficult if not impossible to get healthcare insurance independent of their work. Then there are the years of hardships as they watch their daughter die of AIDS. You bet it's their business.

Kids have the freedom to listen to rap music whose lyrics regularly use the words bitches and whores and preach youth rebellion in general. Kids think that it is their right to listen to this music. The record companies think they have to freedom to produce it. Their excuse is that people do not have to buy it. If they want it then we will produce it. This is the free marketplace. We might call it the freedom market place. It is true that parents do not have to give their kids the money to buy it but with downloads and music copying technology it becomes impossible to keep it from the kids.

These are two examples of our free society.

We now live in a house that was built by the boomers. In future chapters we will examine that house.

Chapter 8

Colleges, the Road to Wealth and Thus Happiness

"A man who has never gone to school may steal from a freight car, but if he has a university education he may steal the whole railroad." Franklin D. Roosevelt

You can't get a good job without a college education, Bill Gates excepted. Who is responsible for that sad state of affairs? Well we can be sure that the colleges are spreading that word. Why? It creates more customers for their business – selling academic credentials.

But they are not the main cause of this phenomenon. When I worked as a manager for the U.S. Government, I often had to write job descriptions. It was well known that you always write a job description so that it requires a college graduate. There are certain keywords that are used for this. The job description must contain words like "decides", "plans", "evaluates", etc. which, presumably, only a college graduate can do.

Since college graduates cost more money then why would one do this? It will run up your salary overhead. Well, first, I said I was working for the government. The taxpayer pays for all of this so what did I care. But there is a more insidious reason. As a manager I can justify a higher pay grade if I am managing college graduates than if I am managing high school graduates. So I wanted nothing but college graduates under me. Everybody in government, at all levels, federal, state, and local plays this game.

Since everyone plays this game, many of the jobs in government do not require a college graduate at all, just a bright high school graduate. But this is one reason people want or perhaps have to go to college. Without the degree many doors are closed by policy.

But the curious thing is that it does not matter in most cases what the degree is in. I ran a computer programming shop. One of my programmers had a degree in Art History. Another had a degree in Sociology. Except in some specialized cases where the job is doing engineering at NASA, for example, it does not matter what the college degree is in. For example, to go to officer school and become an officer in the military, it does not matter what your degree is in, just that you have one.

This phenomenon exists in government at all levels, federal, state, and local. After all, these high salaries are being paid for by the taxpayer. One does not find this to the same extent in the privates sector except in large corporations which have entered the special and most desirable status of "too big to fail." These businesses employ so many people that the government will not allow them to fail, providing loan guarantees and contracts to assure profitability. (Nearly every big company has a division for doing business with the government.) All the automobile companies make things for the defense department. When in trouble the government can throw a few contracts their way to help them out. So one sees this unnecessary college degree requirement in big business also.

Although there are few mom and pop businesses left, one does not see this there. They will ask "can this person do this job?" and forget whether or not they have a college degree It is cheaper to hire a bright high school graduate.

Consulting firms take this to another level. When bidding on work, they want their employee portfolio to show as many

PhDs as possible. Their thinking is that our firm has 10 PhDs while those other guys only have 5 PhDs so we are better qualified to do this consulting work.

All of this makes a college degree nearly mandatory and keeps colleges in business, aided, of course, by government grants to colleges and universities to do studies. When this is done, there is an insinuation by the buyer of the study, the government, as to how they would like to see the study come out. It works like this. We think that there is a correlation between level of income and the amount of assistance that the person got from the government while growing up. We want you to do a study on this. There will be follow on studies depending on the outcome. For those who can read between the lines it goes like this. We want a study that proves that the more government aid you get while growing up, the more money you will make. If your study shows this, you will get follow on contracts to do more studies.

Now you do not have to be a PhD to figure out what your study should conclude. The next time this will come up is when, in a social entitlement bill before Congress, where it will be argued that studies show that the more money we invest in people the higher their income will be and so we will get all that money back in the increased taxes they will pay. The Great Society grows another inch in height.

To that extent colleges and universities are an arm of the government. They are the arm that produces the "independent" studies that justify government behavior.

So the college industry is alive and well. This is naturally a place for Liberals to hang out. First, it is not the real world, a place where Liberals find it hard to function. It's a theoretical based world where nothing is ever settled and much talking goes on. Liberals are particularly good at talking, especially if no conclusion needs to be reached.

You get into this world by staying in school all your life. First high school, then college, then a Master's degree, then a PhD, then you get a job as a college professor and wait for tenure. All along you never had to go into the real world. To add to the glory of it all, you are now considered an expert and called Doctor. What a life, but you do have to pay a lot of money to the education industry. You literally buy this lifestyle with tuition.

But to be fair there are some wonderful college professors who contribute greatly to their field through research and writings so I should not paint them all with the same broad brush. However, I do think that practical experience has its place. For example, how many professors in the School of Business at a university actually had their own business at one time? How many Sociology professors have ever lived in the ghetto?

There is a big issue in the public debate today about the extent to which colleges and universities are too liberal, as in politically liberal. Many college students have complained that if they challenge their liberal professor's views, their grades suffer as a result. Many see colleges as an indoctrination center for the Left. Some colleges and universities don't even try to defend themselves against this charge.

The big attraction that some colleges offer is not education but parties. Some are even known as party schools. Many students find a place to have fun and study the minimum. Agree with the professor so as to get at least a C for the class, do this for 4 years and you get a degree. Then you are all set to go out and make money.

I do not want to take away from or minimize the hard work of the students who work very hard becoming doctors, lawyers and engineers. But simply to point out that some students have it a lot easier than others and where it only matters that you have a degree, why not get the easiest degree possible and have fun at the same time.

A recent change in the college industry is the student loan programs to pay for college. This was unheard of in my day and now about 40% of college kids have student loans. This is because college professors want as much money per annum as they can get. Colleges will argue that to attract good professors they have to pay well. The only way to get this money is to raise tuition and many students can't afford the higher tuitions.

Now if we let the natural market place forces do their job this would take care of itself. If tuition gets too high, kids won't attend that college and shop around for a less expensive college. Suddenly colleges are in competition for students in the way the businesses are in competition for customers. Pressure would be brought to bear to keep college professors' salaries down. The marketplace would do its work.

But remember that I have asserted above that colleges and universities are an arm of the government. The study arm or to some, the propaganda arm. So the government gets into the race with the college loan program to save its propaganda arm.

It sounds so kind. You borrow money from a bank to go to college. We will guarantee that loan, eliminating the bank's risk. When you graduate and start working then you pay the loan back. What a great idea. So what is wrong with that?

What's wrong is that there is a simple economic theory that says that the price of something depends on how much money is available to buy it. By creating the student loan program, the government has made an unlimited amount of money available to pay higher tuitions. So there is no pressure for colleges to hold down their costs. Professor's salaries go through the roof along with tuition cost. Colleges and banks come out big winners.

So who loses? The kids who graduate from college already owing 30 thousand plus dollars have to pay back their student loan. Now under review by Congress, many argue that the student loan program is a better deal for the banking industry than it is for the students. Well for those who know how the world works that does not come as a big surprise.

Many students default on paying back their student loan. Even doctors have been known to do this. When this happens, the government who guaranteed the loan pays the bank back with tax payer dollars. This is now happening so often that the government is setting up reprisals for students who default. They are not eligible for certain government programs, perhaps not eligible for a small business loan for example. This is good but doesn't go far enough. We could withhold their driver's license through an arrangement with the states. That would sure make them pay off the loan.

But there is no real incentive by the Left for such a get tough policy. First, the Left is not a "get tough" bunch of people. Second, all this supports the liberal colleges and their liberal professors who produce all the studies that justify the Left's social programs. So a few default. What's the big deal? The businessmen on the right benefit too as banks make more money. So it is in neither side's interest to stop this practice.

Having a student loan program causes many parents to not see the need to save money for their kid's college tuition. So they like it since they have more money to spend on themselves. Is this a great country or what?

New law will have the federal government simply take over the entire student loan program and cut the banks out all together. Then the IRS can deal with the students who don't pay back their loan.

Under the "equal protection" clause of the Constitution, every American citizen will have a constitutional right to have the federal government to loan them money for college, money that will be collected by the IRS. This will make a virtually unlimited amount of money available to pay professor's salaries and tuitions will soar.

Chapter 9

Jobs Above All Else

"When work is a pleasure, life is a joy. When work is a duty, life is slavery." Maxim Gorky

There came a time in American history where the government took over control of the economy. Before that we had a free economy driven by the marketplace and it was everyone for himself or herself. This had been the model for all human history. The government's role was to simply take a bite for taxes and keep the game fair with laws and regulations.

But this historic process resulted in a boom and bust economy. There were good times followed by bad times in a natural economic cycle. Recessions were common with a depression thrown in from time to time. This process was the result of human nature. When the times were good, selfish businessmen took it too far resulting in a bubble. Soon the bubble burst and the bad times came. But to be fair, weather resulting in droughts played a role. Good weather could result in over production of crops which would lower the price because of over supply and particular markets would crash, often bringing down other markets.

The government, spurred on by the thinking of men like economist Maynard Keynes, who believed in central control of the economy by government, wanted to iron out these wrinkles. They wanted to create a smooth running economy that was recession proof. What they really wanted to eliminate was the public outrage in bad times that often led to a change of government.

Although this sounds like a good idea it overlooks something fundamental. The recessions have a cleansing effect on the economy. Not all businessmen go under during recessions. Not all businessmen overplay their hand causing a bubble. We call these the good businessmen. They survive and the bad businessmen go under. This cleansing effect is a good thing. It forces bad businessmen out of the marketplace leaving more activity for the good businessmen.

Winter serves the same function in nature. During a particularly cold winter, the old, weak and sick animals perish, reducing the population. Then when spring comes there is more food for the survivors who then reproduce in greater numbers. It's all part of a natural cycle. Nature may be cruel, but it works.

By taking control of the economy government removed that cleansing process. So now the bad businessmen survive also. This puts tremendous competitive pressure on everyone and things get ruthless, even vicious. We can make a distinction between healthy competition and vicious competition.

The recent saving of the economy by the government in 2008-2009 had this effect. The same businessmen who caused this gigantic problem are still in power making decisions. The only thing that was saved was the good ol boy network.

So the government, beginning with Roosevelt and the New Deal, began taking control. Earlier, they controlled interest rates by establishing a central bank which we know as the Federal Reserve. By raising interest rates, money that the Federal Reserve loans to banks, things get more expensive and people quit buying so the economy cools off. By decreasing interest rates things get cheaper and people buy more which heats up the economy. This is because most things get purchased with borrowed money and so the interest paid affects the ultimate price paid.

Beyond interest rate control, the American government used to control markets. They would pay farmers not to grow food to keep the profits from food production high, else farmers might go out of business. This fell out of favor when we began exporting our excess. But this has a problem also. Sometimes farmers can make more money exporting their crops than by selling them at home. This is because transportation costs are lower with today's larger ships and the most desperate country will pay the higher price.

Today the government controls the economy by the tax code. By taxing or not, they can control the price of things. We are dependent on oil today because of the Oil Depletion Allowance. Here the argument was made by the oil companies that oil is running out so that massive investments in drilling equipment and refineries would be difficult to justify since the oil is running out. What we need, they argued, is a tax break for our industry to encourage us to make these investments. The Congress fell for that argument and the Oil Depletion Allowance was born.

This made oil and gas cheap but it also made alternate forms of energy more expensive by comparison. Given the tax break for the oil industry, solar energy could not compete. In any cost analyst, it was always cheaper to use oil. To encourage solar energy we would need a Sun Depletion Allowance and curiously the sun is depleting by burning itself up. But there is plenty of sun and as it turns our there is plenty of oil also. It was a grand sham.

There are many examples of Congress using the tax code to eventually determine what is less expensive and what is more expensive. In this sense they control entire industries and the spending habits of the population. Raising money for the government to spend becomes a secondary use of the tax code. Power and control become its primary purpose. The reason is easy to understand. If you are a powerful politician who can have an influence on the tax code, many people will give you campaign contributions to earn favor and gain access to you. If there were, say, a flat tax system with no deductions, many politicians would have a harder time raising money for their campaigns.

Thus the so called Fair Tax is a pipe dream. Figure how many accountants and tax lawyers would be out of a job with the Fair Tax. How many congressmen and senators would lose their power, their power to put in deductions for special interests. And the government would lose the power to control the economy. Fair it may be but the government deals in power and not in fairness.

So what is wrong with the system of the government controlling the economy? It seems to work but we still have recessions, so is it working?

What is wrong in a grand sense is that system of central control causes the voters to think that everything that goes wrong is the government's fault. If I don't have a job, it's Washington's fault. It's not the marketplace's fault and certainly not my fault for not having a better education.

This seems fair since in good times the politicians take credit for it. So then they have to take to blame in the bad times. They do have tremendous control after all. This puts tremendous pressure on politicians to maintain full employment and that goal affects all government decisions as well as foreign policy decisions.

What this represents is a fundamental change in the role of government as envisioned by the Founding Fathers. This is one of the most profound differences in thinking between the Left and the Right. The Right wants less government regulation, less taxes and a more natural marketplace. The Left wants big government, more taxes and a marketplace controlled with government regulations. Their model is that we simply take some money from the rich and give it to the poor. It seems fair but it's as if the rich did not earn the money and thus do not deserve the money. Few, who themselves don't work hard and take risks, don't understand risk taking. Although many people get rich, many people lose everything. And so the rich get penalized.

The problem with the government running the economy is that it becomes a political issue. Vote for me and I will lower taxes. Vote for me and I will increase social security and welfare payments. Vote for me and I will tax the rich. Vote for me and I will create jobs. This is the dialogue that we now hear during elections.

What we should hear and what the Founding Fathers intended that we hear is vote for me and I will create a fair society. Vote for me and there will be justice for all. Vote for me and everyone will have a chance to become anything they want.

So by the government's running the economy, the fundamental nature of our democracy has changed. The most profound change is the idea that it's the government's fault if I don't have a job. This has caused full employment to become the top priority for governments at all levels, federal, state, local. Full employment supersedes justice, fairness, equality and all the things that we traditionally look to government for. It's all about jobs. This leads to some interesting consequences. Here are a few. Beware, this is scary.

Government's job is to solve problems. But problems create jobs. Because of illegal immigration, we are hiring more border patrol agents. Because of home burglaries, an entire industry has been created – home security systems. Because of car theft, there are thousands of people working in the car insurance industry. Because of domestic violence, there are jobs created for thousands of family councilors, psychologists, psychiatrists, etc. I think that is enough examples and you get the point. The real point here is that if those problems go away, so do the jobs of the problem solvers.

Here is what underlines all of this. When a given problem develops, pressure is put on government to solve it. But the marketplace sees an opportunity to offer a solution. In every case the private sector can create a solution, like home security devices, long before the government can go through all the hearings, legislation writing, legislation rewriting, politicking and the like. So during the middle of the giant mess we call legislating, the private sector has already offered a solution for the problem to the public. Now the fun begins for if government finally passes legislation say to increase the punishment for house burglary so harsh that nobody would even consider doing it, then there go all the jobs in the home security industry.

The government politicians and bureaucrats are trying to survive like everything else. When unemployment hits 10-15% they are all out of a job and they know it. They have to keep everybody working at all cost. Have to. And they know full well that solving society's problems with strict punishments will cost jobs. I warned you above that this would be scary.

At this point many readers are thinking that I am paranoid. Well look at the facts. Are punishments lax? Do we still have crime problems? Are most problems solved by the private sector? Is unemployment the biggest issue today? I can get even scarier you want. Consider this. Abortion employs thousands of doctors. The Iraqi war creates thousands of jobs in the defense industry. Illegal immigration creates jobs everywhere including in the all important legal profession. Crime in general creates jobs for policemen, lawyers, judges, prison guards, probation officers, councilors, security camera manufacturers, security alarm manufacturers and I have only scratched the surface. Crime is the biggest industry in America. We don't know that because it is not tracked as an industry and overall statistics are not reported that way. If crime magically went away we would have a super depression as all those people lost their jobs.

Spam and computer viruses create jobs. There are entire companies created to control spam and viruses. Many software products are available for purchase. This is why we won't stop spam and viruses.

The governor of our state recently signed a bill into law that reduces the number of convictions for car theft from 7 to 3 before there will be any jail time. Imagine that, you have to be convicted 3 times for car theft before you go to jail. This is good news for the car theft insurance industry. If the law was that you go to jail for 20 years on the first offense, there would be little car thievery going on. This would reduce the demand for car theft insurance. But imagine it used to be 7 offenses in my state. Of course, car theft was rampant, and much done by repeat offenders. Car theft insurance was very costly. This means that car theft insurance companies were very prosperous.

In the wild west horse stealing was a hanging offense and was relatively rare. Suppose there had been horse insurance. Somebody steals your horse, the insurance company gives you money to buy another horse. Horse stealing would not have been a hanging offense. This is why little happens to those who steal cars today. Car theft supports an entire industry employing thousands of people. Remember the government's top priority is full employment.

In the legislative process in Congress, with all the hearings and arguments for and against the legislation, how many jobs will be created or lost is always the issue. The worst of legislation will pass if it creates a significant number of jobs and the best of legislation will fail to pass if it eliminates jobs. Jobs created or lost becomes a major criteria for voting on legislation.

So the process was simple. To smooth out the natural raise and falls in the economy, government took control. This eliminated the natural cleansing effect that was good for the economy as government controlled interest rates, manipulated natural economic activity with the tax code. This caused people to blame the government for their economic problems. This caused politicians to change the political dialogue when running for office, running on maintaining full employment. This reduced the efforts to solve problems by government action, rather to merely leave it up to the marketplace.

In economic theory economics is based on needs. People need things and so other people make these things and sell or trade them. This creates a market place that runs on its own, self-governing. When the price of things go up, you make more of them. When people stop buying your product, you quit making it. An equilibrium develops. A self- regulating economy.

The only role for government in this self-regulating world we call the marketplace is to keep things fair. The government is like a referee at a ball game. Not to take sides, and not to play in the game but to see that the play is fair. It's legitimate for the government to outlaw dishonest advertising for example.

But sadly, people are cheated by the thousands in the market place each day. Frauds, scams are rampant. So where is the government? There are busy worrying how many jobs would be lost if they cracked down on things. After all, the rule of the market place is *caveat emptor*, let the buyer beware. It's curious that we don't have a catchy phrase for let the voter beware.

So we have a situation in recent history where the government only goes through the motions of performing its legitimate roll as referee while vigorously pursuing its questionable or at least debatable role of guaranteeing that everyone has a job so the politicians can stay in power.

Of course, full employment also creates more tax revenue for them to spend to buy votes.

But now they are in a real fix. Recent trade agreements, curiously entered into to create jobs in America, have made it possible to find cheaper labor overseas. So rather than creating jobs in America, jobs are being shipped offshore to find this cheap labor. The jobs are not actually shipped off shore. What happens is that a company needs a million, say, widgets. They announce this to the world and a company with cheap labor can under bid everyone so the widgets get made in that country and not in America where the widget will cost more. The lowest bidder gets the job.

Trade deficits occur when we do business with other countries. It works like this. We buy something from, say, Japan. This gives the Japanese dollars to buy something from us. If they buy more goods and services from us than we buy from Japan, a trade deficit occurs. They have a stockpile of dollars to spend. In the 70's there was a great scare when the Japanese began buying whole American companies, our prize golf courses and hotels, movie studios and skyscrapers. It looked like Japan was buying America and the public was greatly concerned. Today China could do that if they wished but dollars can be used to buy anything in the world. So rather than buy up America and annoy the American people, they can buy up assets of other countries.

We are running a trade deficit with nearly everyone we trade with. But not to worry. The rich are getting richer. That part is working fine. America has 40% of the world's billionaires.

That global economy plan sure backfired if it was sincerely meant to work in the first place. Also, the plethora of welfare programs and safety nets created by the Great Society have created a class of citizen that will not do certain jobs. Thus Mexican labor, legal and illegal, is flooding to America to do the jobs that "Americans won't do." What are these jobs? Well picking fruits and vegetables for one. It seems that Blacks in the fields picking vegetables would bring back images of slaves in the South working in the fields and we can't have that. Better to have unemployment insurance and welfare. Only in America do the poor not work in the fields. Every where else that is their job. In many countries prisoners work in the fields. But we can't have that either, that would be cruel and unusual punishment and compete with private labor. Using prisoners would cost jobs in the private sector.

So we are in a pickle trying to keep everyone employed, now the chief role of government. It has a grand effect on our thinking as a society. And we have an opponent in this fight. It's technology. As hard as we are working to keep everyone employed, there are people working just as hard to put people out of work, to replace them with machines. Each machine is sold by showing that in, say, 3 years of a person's labor cost, you could pay for the machine.

Throughout history technology has been putting people out of work or, better said, changing the nature of the work they do. Machines can now work the fields in many cases. Robots build cars in Detroit. Electronics are built by robots.

It is said that those put out of work can build the machines but that simplistic view doesn't always work. Usually the person put out of work does not have the skills to build machines. So, then we will set up trade schools to retrain them.

Well remember that the reason they are doing menial labor in the first place is because they did not do well in school. So why would they do better in trade school. In many cases they do not have the foundation in math and science to perform well in trade schools and work with modern technology.

So they usually go to another menial job, say from harvesting potatoes, now done by machine, to flipping burgers. Thus, the challenge is to create menial jobs. We are getting good at that. The labor force needs people to run check out registers, stock shelves, unload trucks and flip burgers. Ironically, our school systems which no longer provides a quality education to most, does teach kids enough to do these menial jobs. In that sense the school systems work.

Many jobs, like stamping out metal parts for cars is now done overseas where there is cheap labor and no unions. But we do have a lot of engineering jobs left. But these require a college degree. Even these quality jobs can be done overseas with the Internet and e-mail where specs and engineering drawings can be sent around the world in seconds.

The notion of jobs above else explains other things. For example, why are we building B-1 bombers, supersonic fighters, nuclear submarines and aircraft carriers when there is no one to fight. We are the only superpower left. Well first, building these things keeps people in the arms industry employed. But there is a certain logical aspect to this beyond jobs. Few countries have companies that can build a nuclear submarine or a supersonic fighter. Few countries have the technology. We are lucky in that we have companies that can do this.

Given that we do not know what the future holds, we might need to have these companies in the future. But to keep these companies in business we have to give them contracts to build arms. Suppose that we stopped building nuclear submarines.

The company that builds them would go out of business. They would sell off their facilities, their engineers would get other jobs as would their labor force - shipwrights, welders, etc. Now suppose the world situation changes and suddenly we need nuclear submarines. We have a problem. It would take a long time to put that company back together. We would have to start from scratch, acquire land for the shipyard, rebuild the facilities, recruit engineers and labor. We would not get the same people, people who had hands on experience in successfully doing this. There would be a lot of training involved.

It might take years to get back to the level we were at. Easier is to keep these existing companies, a national asset, alive by throwing them a contract from time to time. This also keeps people employed. Often when companies go under the employees do not find a job that pays the same. They often make less and so pay less taxes. Once burned and resettled, few would want to go back into that again. So we buy military weapons and the public does not understand why.

The same is true for NASA. Having created it why would we want to destroy it. So we explore space, while as some say, we should be spending that money here on Earth rather than exploring Mars. True to some extent but we are lucky to have a NASA and the Hubble telescope. How many countries can boast a NASA? And technology comes out of NASA that has applications in many areas of the civilian economy.

But as could be predicted, there is a lot of waste in both NASA and the defense industries. One may recall the $400 toilets seats uncovered by the Reagan administration. An interesting story is that fact that NASA discovered that ball pens would not work in zero gravity. We spent millions developing a ball point pen that would write in zero gravity. The Russians? They used pencils in space.

But one man's waste is another man's income. This is true of pork barrel spending by the Congress and government waste in general. The money is not being wasted, it's being used to create jobs. The billions spent on the Iraqi war is not being spent in the Iraqi economy, its being spent in the American economy to build weapons for the war. Those billions are employing millions of Americans. Could that money be better spent in other areas? Well that depends. Do we want to have engineers who know how to build weapons? If that money is spent elsewhere like in social programs, then it will employ social workers, psychologists, councilors and the like. Soon we would have fewer engineers and an excess of social workers.

Jobs go where the money is. By the way when the government spends its money, it creates jobs in certain professions. Want more engineers in society, then spend more money on defense. Want more social workers in society, then spend more money on social programs.

There is a giant balancing act that takes place in Congress of which the general public is totally unaware. It creates jobs and it creates professions. Now this is far from a natural economy free of government control. But the private sector is not going to start a space program. It doesn't have the capital nor is there any evidence that they will make their investment back. Knowing what Mars looks like does not make anybody any money.

But eventually, once the kinks are worked out, the private sector takes over. Private companies now build and launch satellites for profit. The government, at the same time creating jobs, thereby reducing unemployment and keeping the same politicians in office, is stimulating future economic growth. So the issue is not black and white. Waste? Sure but this waste is someone's income. And it's all about jobs.

One interesting way that the government stimulates the economy and creates jobs is with tax rebates. From time to time the government gives everyone a $300 or $400 tax rebate. A check is sent in the mail to all tax payers. Does this create jobs? Well it depends on what the public spends the money on. If they buy the latest electronics, which are made overseas now, then all we do is increase the balance of payments with those countries by buying their production. If the money is spent buying American made goods, then it will create more jobs in America. But the government can't tell people how to spend their money, even the money that the government gives the public.

Chapter 10

The New American Culture

"Culture, the acquainting ourselves with the best that has been known and said in the world"- Matthew Arnold

It is being called America's Idiot Culture and there are perfectly logical reasons how it came about. By culture I am referring to music, movies, books and TV shows primarily although technically, the word culture is more encompassing than that.

Our culture was once renown throughout the world. We invented the movie as an art form. We invented Jazz and Blues as music forms or genres. We invented TV shows.

Early American cultural expressions in these art forms were magnificent. The big band music of World War II was listened to around the world.

What is being called the decline possibly started with modern art. Suddenly what was being promoted as art were pictures that had to subject, no perspective, and no clever use of light and shadowing. Actually this may have started with Picasso and his friends.

This was quickly followed by poetry that did not have to rhyme and have meter. Indeed, what was previously true about any art form in the past was not a requirement for that art form in the future. Anyone could call themselves a poet, sculptor or a painter.

Now I have no particular problem with this since I realize that art culture grows and changes throughout history.

Furthermore, we do not have to look at it or listen to it. But I confess that it does annoy me that a person can call himself a painter, placing himself with the great painters of history, who can't draw a reasonable horse when asked. Picasso who promoted cubism could draw quite well in the traditional sense.

So I use this test. You show me a painting you made by throwing paint filled balloons at the canvas. Then I will ask you to draw a horse. If you draw a reasonable horse, I will accept your painting as art. If you can't, I will tell you not to bore me with absurdity masquerading as art nor to call yourself an artist in my presence.

The culture mostly being discussed today is the culture enjoyed by our children, specifically hip hop music, TV shows like MTV, computer games and movies. Some say that this is actually harmful to kids. Sex and violence are everywhere. Computer games have a program setting about how real do you want this to look. At max violence when you shoot a character, his head explodes, blood and brains everywhere. At lower violence settings he just falls down. Which setting do you suppose the kids chose? But this culture, too, is being sold around the world.

A potential problem is that many people are confusing TV with reality. Many young people think that what they see on TV is how things work. Let's take CSI. Somebody dies and for the next hour we see all the scientific tests being done to figure out who killed them. A very good show but that does not happen every time somebody is killed. You would get the impression that all this work takes place and that every murder is solved. That is far from the case.

You may remember the FBI with Efrem Zimbalist Jr. He was clean cut and the FBI agents were professionals. Yet we know what J. Edgar Hoover was up to regarding Martin Luther King Jr. while this show was running.

Perhaps you remember the movie The Green Berets staring that American of Americans John Wayne. It came out during the Viet Nam war. We now know that we were losing that war all along but the movie gave us the impression that we were winning and more importantly that it was a good war. We were supposed to think that this is how the Viet Nam war was going.

So first, the entertainment industry has become a propaganda arm of the government even though they have no control over it. They do go out of their way to protect the speech found there. But the people who do control the industry are sympathetic to the Left. Not only does much entertainment support the Left but it often attacks the Right.

When the Nazis were doing this to the German people and the Communists were doing this to the Russian people we were calling it propaganda and brainwashing. Today we call it entertainment protected by the First Amendment.

Most changes regarding the new American culture can be traced to new technology. Take the laugh box. Someone invented an electronic box that produces laughter. Before that, comedy shows were filmed before a live audience. That was the only way to get laughter. But there is a problem with that system – the joke has to be funny or no one will laugh. This means that you need good writers and they cost money. With the laugh box the laughter is supplied after the punch line even if the joke is not funny. This laughter, like a yawn, is supposed to make you laugh too.

It's easy to recognize shows where a laugh box is being used. First, the laughter all sounds the same and second, there is laughter even when the joke is not funny. With this invention, comedy shows went downhill fast. Poor writing, cheap jokes offered as entertainment.

This replaced such shows as Sid Caesar's Show of Shows. Presented live, the jokes and skits had to be funny or no one would laugh.

Other technology changes are the ability to create explosions through animation. We see whole buildings explode and violent car crashes. Kids love this stuff but for adults it gets boring after a while. But it is entertaining to some and the movies are filled with it.

The chief change in entertainment is its focus on sex. There are shows like "Sex in the City", Desperate Housewives and "the Real Housewives of Orange County". The titles themselves are suggestive. I wonder what the women's movement thinks about this?

So why does this happen? Well sex sells especially to kids who are exploring sex. There used to be programming standards and practices. There were actually network censors and much was forbidden. But as one network relaxed their standards and allowed more risqué stuff on TV, the other networks, competing as they do, were forced to relax their standards also. Soon there was a race to the bottom underway. There was and is a race for viewers so what ever got people to watch was acceptable. Viewers equal advertising sales which creates profits for the network, and it all about profits. Recall that the boomers had moved up and into decision making positions by then.

We have a ways to go before TV shows become pornographic but we are headed in that direction. But there is "girls gone wild". One of the tenets of the women's movement was that women were treated like sex objects. Has the women's movement sold out?

It has gotten so bad that the onus had been placed on parents who can now block certain shows as being too violent or having too much sexual content for their kids. This is a good approach given that the networks have abandoned their responsibilities with their standards and practices.

The check used to be that sponsors did not want their name or product associated with the show. In the early days of TV shows were sponsored by one company. Texaco sponsored Milton Berle. Carnation (condenser milk) sponsored Gracie Allen. Every big company had a show which they sponsored. They wanted that show to be good since their product and company was associated with it.

Then the networks started encouraging multiple advertisers for a show as advertising spots grew in length.. Today, a given show has many sponsors so the no particular sponsor is associated with the show and its content. Some sponsors do refuse to sponsor some shows but it is becoming rarer. For most it becomes a matter of how many people watch this show and what does a 30 second spot cost. Demographics play a role. If it is a show watched by young people, then people who sell products directed at the young will buy a spot for advertising. You can count on these shows having a lot of sex and violence.

This multiple sponsor approach has another advantage. There is only so much that one sponsor can say during a commercial break. One sponsor could not have a 5 minute commercial. But 5 sponsors could each have a 1 minute commercial making a 5 minute commercial break. Thus commercial breaks could be longer making even more money for the network. The ratio of commercial time to program time is steadily increasing. The public gets used to this trend if it happens slowly enough. So more commercial breaks are being slipped in. Often there is a commercial for the show being interrupted during the commercial break, saying "we'll be right back. Then, more commercials.

Under this system there is not as much emphasis on how good the show is by any individual sponsoring company. This is a major change as it generally removes the sponsor from the loop and puts the writers in charge. Everyone is protected by the 1st Amendment and they all argue that people do not have to watch. We run it because the public wants to watch it is the thinking. "This is the freedom that we have today" is the message from the Left.

And to be fair it does sell and even sells overseas when it is not censored. It's quite a deference in programming from that of, say, England and its availability via satellite makes it difficult to stop. So not only are we corrupting our youth, we are corrupting the youth of the world with much of our new culture. Some call us the Great Satan.

But that it sells should not be the measurement criteria, nor should the criteria be that it entertains. Pornography sells and is entertaining to some. That does not necessarily make pornography a good thing. In this regard, the Supreme Court recently made an interesting decision. They ruled that child pornography was illegal only if it involved a real child. It was the use of the real child that was illegal. If, for example, a child pornographic movie was in cartoon form or used computer graphics to show the adult/child acts, then it was protected by the 1st amendment. What is troubling about this decision is that computer graphics and scenes rendered by computers is getting more and more lifelike. Soon it will be hard to tell the difference. Plus it is getting cheaper and cheaper to do.

So we can expect an explosion of child pornography in the future. This will extend to bestiality as well. This will not be on TV but will be easily downloaded from the Internet which means it will be available to curious children as well as the adults who are willing to pay for it.

This is reminiscent of the Roman Empire. Sex was everywhere and the games at the coliseum were very violent indeed. Real people fought and were killed by lions in front of the crowds The Roman people could not seem to get enough of it. And of course they collapsed strangely because their army was too soft to repel invaders.(See chapter 15 - The Softening Military) How could the military of such a violent people get so soft?

Well, like us, they probably confused show time with reality. Many Americans think that what they see on TV is the way the world really works. It sure looks real. Seeing the combat in the arena possibly made the average Roman think that this is what would happen to their enemies if they were invaded.

When we watch our military in the movies it is hard to understand why we are losing the war in Afghanistan or how we lost the Viet Nam war. It the movies we look unbeatable. Perhaps the Romans thought they were unbeatable too.

So both TV and the movies are generally unreal. Lately there is reality TV. This is real and popular and even entertaining which is all it has to be to make money. But it is not real in the sense that it is staged. Today's reality shows generally set up a situation and a script and films what happens.

Our music culture has changed greatly. In the 50's there we show tunes and some popular music. Tony Bennett, Frank Sinatra and Dean Martin were big stars. Then came Rock and Roll. Initially black music featuring Little Richard, Fats Domino, Chubby Checker and Chuck Berry and was very crude as music goes. Most songs had 3 chords and followed a format as regards verses and choruses. But the rock genre had not developed. Its height was probably Sgt. Pepper by the Beatles. The form evolved into a wonderful art form that was musically sophisticated and remains so for a long time. That was certainly the golden era of popular music. Today's rap music, though still evolving, leaves a lot to be desired when compared to 60's and 70's music. But to be fair it is still evolving. It started as rhythmic poetry to a drum beat. And that is a valid art form in the same sense that modern art is a valid art form and poetry that does not rhyme is a valid art form.

The problem for rap music's evolution is that it will evolve into 60's music. By dropping everything but lyrics and a drum beat, there is no other choice than to put this back in as the evolution takes place. Indeed, music itself evolved from jungle drum beat and chants into Mozart and Beethoven. Visual art evolved from drawings in caves and on pottery to the Dutch masters.

So I expect to see rap add first bass, then an accentuated half beat, then melody and harmony and become what popular music has always been. The message in any popular song is in its lyrics. There is no limit to where that can go. But lyrics are not music, lyrics are poetry. To be music there has to be music involved. In that sense, having removed everything musical in rap, the only evolutionary choice is to put that stuff back in. It's the only way to distinguish your music from the rest, a thing all musicians strive for. Making your lyrics different from the rest is easy to achieve since all music's lyrics can be and are different as regards the words themselves Compare the lyrics of the Beatles with the lyrics of Bob Dylan.

Dance too has evolved from grand ballroom dancing and waltzes to two people standing in front of each other shaking their bodies in a sexual, provocative way. Dancing seems to have hit rock bottom, morally speaking with freak dancing or freaking as the kids call it. This is often done at school dances. Here the girl bends over and the guy approaches her from behind as if entering into the doggie style of sexual intercourse. They wiggle around often as school officials look on. In some places it is forbidden by the school. This is easy to fix. Just film the dance and send copies to the girl's father to show him his daughter in action.

We are witnessing an evolution of art forms. There has always been this evolution. The question is will this art appeal to the better angels of our nature or hasten our moral decline.

Chapter 11

The New Plantation

"There they are cutting each other's throats, because half of them prefer hiring their servants for life, and the other by the hour." Thomas Carlyle on the American Civil War

Another grand change that has occurred in recent American history is the workplace

When I entered the workplace in 1960 (I worked my way through college) it looked like this.

The whole place was run by men, women being mothers who stayed at home and raised their children or worked mostly as secretaries. You worked for 7 1/2 hours and got an hour for lunch. You got healthcare insurance and two weeks paid vacation a year. There was paid sick leave for everyone. If you happened to be on call after normal work hours, you got paid extra for it. In general, once you got home you could forget work. If you happened to be sent on a business trip, the travel days were not work days but more like vacation days. You could leave your job for another anytime you wanted. This scenario describes at least 90% of the professional employee jobs. The only professional people who were exempt from this were the people who had their own businesses. Like today, they generally worked all the time.

I call today's workplace a plantation because the plantation was a workplace itself. It is interested to compare the workplace described above with the workplace of the slave and then with the workplace of today.

Slaves worked from sun up until sun down about 12 hours a day. They were provided with a place to live and food to eat. This was actually their pay. They could not leave their place of employment. There was no vacation, no official sick leave, no professional health care and no overtime.

To be fair it should be pointed out that most slave owners took care of their slaves. They were valuable property and except for those babies who were born on the plantation and grew up to be worker slaves, slaves were acquired at great expense. A slave might cost $2000. When you pay that kind of money for something, you don't beat it to death else you would lose your $2000. Slaves that were born there had a value too. Many slaves were traded. So you did not beat them to death either. If a slave got sick it was in your interest that they did not spread a communicable disease to the other slaves and that they got well so they could go back to work.

So here are two workplaces, the slave plantation and the workplace which I entered in 1960. Now I describe another workplace which I call the new plantation. This is the workplace in America today.

First, you don't get an hour for lunch. That was necessary because it might take an hour to go to the lunch counter at the drugstore and get served. The same is true for the local restaurant. Some people did bring their lunch but they got an hour also. Time for a walk in the park or some lunch time shopping. It was called your lunch hour.

Then the fast food restaurant was born. Now you can get a burger in 5 minutes, eat it in 5 minutes. So why do you need an entire lunch hour. The lunch hour became a half hour for most people. Thus, many people don't really come back from lunch refreshed. Some employees are worked so hard that they eat at their desk. There is plenty of coffee, usually free, since coffee is a stimulant and makes you work harder.

The work day is still 7 ½ to 8 hours but you don't forget about work when you get home. Everyone has beepers, cell phones and often supplied laptop computers by the company. You are actually on call 24 hours a day but you don't get extra pay for that anymore. Most people are expected to check their messages and email even when not at work. Most people are beepable to answer questions anytime. Many people, given the fierce competition in today's workplace, take their laptop home and do work at home. So in summary many people work at least 10 hours a day just like the slaves did.

Overtime still exists for labor and those in unions. But the workplace has identified the professional or managerial worker. These people are expected to work extra for no extra money. Many people stay after normal work hours to catch up and they don't get paid for it.

On travel days you are expected to work on the plane. Take your laptop, reports, etc. and use that time productively. You are getting paid for that day after all. That you are being dragged away from your home and family is beside the point.

Healthcare still exists for those working for large companies, but 40% of uninsured Americans have a full time job. Healthcare is now too expensive for most small companies to be able to afford it. (See the chapter on healthcare for the reasons). So many people do not have healthcare except in the emergency rooms of the hospital. Many workers do not get paid sick leave, forcing them to come to work when sick and giving the flu to co-workers.

The final point to be made here is that many people are as chained to their current workplace as slaves were chained to theirs. Many people do not have the freedom to find another job. Why? Well if they have healthcare insurance at their current job, they will need a job that also offers equivalent healthcare insurance. This eliminates small business and eliminates starting your own business, the dream of many people. Private healthcare cost at least $700 a month if you qualify. If anyone in your family has, say, diabetes, you may not qualify. A great many people can't change jobs simply because the healthcare keeps them chained to their current job. Big corporations offer the best healthcare and thus have their pick of employees.

This actually has a negative effect on the entire economy. People are more productive when they are happy. They might be happier and thus more productive in another job, say, with a small business. But the small business may not offer healthcare so they are stuck being less happy and thus less productive in their current job. Multiply that loss of productivity by, say, 50 million people and it adds up fast. National healthcare might increase overall productivity.

So many people are chained to their job, working all the time just like slaves were. This is why I call this the new plantation. And the stress is far greater.

There has been a tremendous change from the workplace I entered in the 60's to today's workplace and yet we still brag about being the richest country in the world. Check out the benefits of the German worker. They get a full month off each year and complete healthcare wherever they work and they lost the war. The Japanese worker is in a similar situation and they lost the war as well.

Our leaders dismiss this as socialism and say that we are practicing the better system, capitalism. When I was in South Korea for 4 months and you pull into a gas station, you are bombarded with people filling your car, checking your oil, cleaning you wind shield and there is always a little gift. It used to be that way in America but now I am expected to do all this myself. Imagine that I live in the richest country and I have to pump my own gas. What is wrong with this picture?

In a marketplace with little government control, a system like the following would develop. A few unemployed kids would hang around the gas station. When a car came in they would pump the gas, clean the windshield, check the oil and handle the payment while you stayed in the air conditioned car. For this you would tip the kid a dollar. The unemployed kid could make at least $20 a day doing this, maybe more. There is value added to the gas station whose customers would be happy not to have to drag that hose around and get dirty checking their oil. This would be a great system benefiting everyone. So why has this not developed?

Well first, the liberal lawyers from the Left would make the case that the kid is actually an employee of the gas station. As such the owner must pay him the minimum wage, deduct his Social Security payments, pay his unemployment insurance and his workman's compensation. All of this is beyond the station owner's ability to pay and so we pump our own gas while the kids remain unemployed. But it does keep alive the issue and problem of unemployed youth. This is grist for the mill of the social reformers who think that government should solve this problem and not the marketplace. As I have said before in this book, they have to keep these problems alive.

But there is another set of chains that keep many people on the plantation. These are chains of their own making but chains none the less. This is their debt, particularly their credit card debt.

Changing jobs when under great debt is a risky proposition. You know where you stand with your current job but what about your new job. Can you do it? Will you be successful? Will the company be successful? If you guess wrong and get laid off you could be in big trouble.

As I said these chains of your own making but you had some help. First, there are unsolicited credit cards. You open the mail and suddenly you have $5000 available balance on this credit card, which you did not ask for. Just use it and it's activated. Who would not stick it in their wallet? Who knows you may need it someday. Now it's in your wallet along with the other ones you may have gotten in the mail. The point is here that you did not ask for this temptation. Now you are loaded.

Now you are bombarded with TV and other commercials. There are three types of commercials. The first, product availability commercials, simply say that here is a new product on the market and here is what it does. These are good else we would never know about new products. The second are comparative commercials. They say here is our product and ours is better than theirs. Ours does this and theirs won't do this. This was not allowed in the 50's. This is where Brand X came from. Then you could not mention the other product by name only as Brand X. The law was changed and now you can mention the very name of your competitor's product. But if you lie, you will find yourself in court.

The third and most dangerous commercial is the recent, as I call it, loser commercial. These commercials are designed to make you feel like a loser if you don't have one of these. There are typically two people, one handsome or beautiful and one ugly. The ugly one, the loser, is poorly dressed when compared to the cute one who is the winner. The loser does not have their product and the winner does. You want to be a winner don't you? Well then buy this product. These commercials appeal to the fact that everyone wants to be a winner thus must have one of these. There is the guy who watches the ball game on the small TV while the winner has the new big screen TV. Everybody is at his house while the loser is all alone.

I call these dangerous because the attack the psyche of the American public. It's little more than brain washing.

Add to this the fact that everyone gets depressed or down from time to time often because of their job pressure and stress, office politics and the resulting unfairness and their jerk boss, and there you are feeling down, in a big store with a $5000 available balance on the unsolicited credit card in your wallet. And what is before you? A big screen TV. The next thing you have to decide is where you put it when you get it home and the game party you will give this weekend. Suddenly, you feel up again and on top of the world. This is actually addictive. Every time you snort coke you feel great at least for a while. Every time you buy something, you feel great, at least for a while. Another snort or another purchase will bring you up again.

Then there is this scenario. With both parents working, they often do not have quality time to be with the kids. Quality time is when you are not worn out from the traffic on the way home and the hard day you had with all the stress. All you really want to do is lay on the sofa and watch the big screen TV. But there are the kids with their demands for your time.

Many parents have taken to showing their kids love by buying them something that they want like the Ipod or the Xbox or the latest cell phone. And here you are with an available balance on the unsolicited credit card in your wallet.

This is why I said that you had help putting those chains around your neck but again they are chains none the less. Soon you find yourself with $20,000 on the balances of your unsolicited credit cards and changing jobs becomes a risky thing to do. You are stuck on the plantation.

Finally, I want to touch on a very sensitive subject – women in the workplace. I worked in the workplace when there were no women apart from clerical workers and I worked in the workplace when there were women Vice Presidents. I will tell you that they were different workplaces. In meetings with all men we could curse, talk frankly and not worry about hurting anyone's feelings.

Add one women to the meeting and the social dynamic changes. Manners become important especially when speaking to her. Bad language is out. I think the meetings are less effective.

We see this with kids as well. It part of human nature. Take 5 high school boys hanging out talking. Everything is fine regarding the relationships. Then add one pretty girl to the mix. Right away the relationships between the boys change. A male ordering is now necessary. Who is the alpha male becomes important. If two boys think themselves to be the alpha male, then tension develops. Before the appearance of the female it did not matter. Now all of a sudden a hierarchy is required among the boys. Add another female of similar looks and a female competition arises. The whole dynamic of the group changes. This is true of meetings in the workplace as well and for the same reasons. Its causes lie in primitive reactions between the sexes. Add to this the complexity of who works for who and you have a very complex social dynamic.

When a woman or man sees a person of the opposite sex and they are attractive, they immediately have a sexual thought. It is nature and totally involuntary. Often pleasant words are exchanged maybe even some innocent flirting. When you are the man and the cute woman is a secretary there is no problem, at least for the man. When you are the man and the woman, cute or not, is a Vice President and your boss, this is a different matter. The last thing you want to do is reject your boss,

Often these innocent relationships can grow into an outright pass. If she makes it and she is your boss you are in big trouble. The same is true if your are the boss and she is a secretary but that case has always existed in the workplace. Many women have filed sexual harassment law suits against their boss. What has changed is that she may be your boss now. Naturally, every body wants to get ahead so what happens if she makes a pass at you?

When you reject her she has a problem. She has to prove to you that that was not a pass. To do that she has to show you that she doesn't even like you. So there begins the meetings that your should have gone to but were not invited. There are the business trips that you should have gone on but were not invited. Then there are the difficult projects that are assigned to you. Often you will get embarrassed in a meeting in front of your peers. Soon you will form the opinion that that was not a pass, she doesn't even like me.

So there are issues in this new workplace. The same things occur in the military where men and women are put into close quarters.

Now there is a new plantation and plantation is not too strong a word to use. So many people are shackled to their boring job with a boss they can't stand by debt or healthcare insurance. They live a life of lonely desperation.

This causes many people to start their own business. It is, in fact, a dream that many people have. People do it everyday but many fail. The first problem is where do you get the money for start up? Bankers will tell you to get it off your credit cards and borrow it from your fiends and relatives. Many do. But beyond start up money there are other problems. First, will be credit. Once you quit your paying job for your own business few people will extend you credit.

Then there is healthcare. How do you pay for healthcare for your family while you are establishing your business. Many people can't do this merely because they can't afford healthcare for their families. Also, how do you attract employees if you can't offer them healthcare? The healthcare system is like golden handcuffs keeping you in place. In many cases the wife works a menial job just to get the healthcare for her family while her husband is starting his business.

But if those problems are overcome, then you have to be prepared to work 16 hours a day and self-employed businessmen regularly do this. It can be fun but you have to have a lot of experience in the business you are trying to start.

Once there were mom and pop businesses everywhere. Then came the computer and "point of sales inventory." Point of sales inventory systems automatically keep up with what is being sold when it is scanned and the computer automatically reorders when stock get low. But this technology allows a few people do the reordering for, say 1000 stores or even 10,000 stores. So the chain store was born putting moms and pops out of business. This is because with all this centralized management and large volume buying, small stores can't remain competitive. Their prices will always be higher and they will go under. This is the economic model that allows WalMart, K Mart, Home Depot, etc. to make more products available at cheaper prices. This even applies to restaurants and fast food places who can take advantage of volume discount buying.

All that is needed on the new plantation is people to stock the shelves and people to run the checkout counters – all minimum wage jobs. Everything else is done at headquarters. So more and more people work for large corporations when these people used to have their own businesses like local restaurants, hardware stores and appliance stores.

Technology has always been the driving force behind civilization. Small farmers are being replaced by agribusinesses, small stores being replaced by chain stores which makes everyone an employee. As everyone becomes an employee, a new kind of worker becomes prevalent - the sycophant.

It turns out that it is easier to get ahead by being close to the boss than by producing. Out producing your peers will tend to cause your peers to organize against you. For example, there is often an heir-apparent. This is the person who it is understood will get the boss' job when to boss retires or gets promoted. Sensing this, people are already starting to suck up to the heir-apparent. Then comes a high producer. If producing is the way to get ahead then why shouldn't this person get the boss' job? The heir-apparent is threatened and those suck ups around him will spring into action. It will be the high producer against his peers. Suddenly and magically, the high producer does not look like a team player – a thing today that you have to be above all else on the new plantation. The word goes out that, sure, he is a high producer but he can't work with people. The sycophants spring into action to save the heir-apparent.

This happens because the boss too is in a highly competitive environment. What the boss needs is loyal people around him. These people are called team players. They are on the boss' team and help the boss compete with his peers. There are spies who report back what they have heard. There are snitches who tell on people. There are double agents as well. It gets very complex especially in governments and large corporations. Political infighting is every where. One wonders how they manage to produce a product but remember, governments do not produce a product. This activity reaches a fever pitch if word of a reorganization hits the rumor mill. Everybody becomes a sycophant in hopes of protecting their position and thus their salary.

American Heritage dictionary defines a sycophant as – "A servile [cravenly submissive] self-seeker who attempts to win favor by flattering influential people." Well that's how the dictionary defines it but we often compose in our minds the meaning of words by what we see. Our minds often recognize concepts that we do not know the official word for.

You should know these words because you are surrounded by sycophants in the new plantation. You know the type. We used to call them brown-nosers. We often call them ass-kissers or suck ups. Critical to the definition of sycophant is the notion that is that the people whom they are flattering are people of power, particularly people who have power over them like the boss.

These are people who laugh at the boss' jokes especially if the joke is not funny. These people always agree with the boss even if they know that he/she is wrong. If an employee questions the boss even with subtlety, the sycophant sees this as a suck up opportunity and attacks the questioner, thereby making points with the boss by coming to his/her defense.

For them the boss is always right. They take every opportunity to flatter the boss and attack those whom they think the boss does not like. They are the boss' boy they let it be known that the boss can always count on them. Powerful men are surrounded by many sycophants.

So how can you recognize the sycophants? It's easy. They are the ones who always get the promotion. They get the window office that has recently become available. When there are layoffs, they don't get laid off. When there is a re-organization, they get better jobs. It seems that sycophancy works. All they have to do to sleep at night is to use one of several accepted rationales. 1) Everybody does it. 2) I have a family to support and I do what I have to. Soon they are snoozing away, financially safe and secure, except for that little voice that never goes away.

One theory of the causes of the decline of empires is that the tipping point comes when a majority of citizens become sycophants. Then no one challenges the boss or the leadership. No one speaks truth to power. Powerful men both in government and Corporate America go on unchecked, indeed encouraged by those who surround them. In our recent history President Lyndon Johnson was known to have been the least tolerant of having his decisions questioned by well-meaning subordinates.

Once Bill Moyers, who was an aid to President Johnson and at the Johnson ranch, was asked where President had gone. Bill said "I saw him by the lake." "Is he walking by the lake" he was asked. "No, he is walking on the lake" Bill replied in jest. When word of that remark got back to Johnson, via a sycophant no doubt, Bill Moyers was gone. He started a career in public television.

This is an important word to know because knowing it explains so many things including why nothing ever changes. Everyone is afraid to challenge power, especially in these days where everyone is carrying so much debt – chains of their own making. If most people miss a couple of pay checks, they are in big trouble. Better to keep your mouth shut. Better still is to flatter the boss at every opportunity and always attack anyone who challenges the boss however subtly. Bankers by handing out unsolicited credit cards which they knew would be used, have changed the very nature of society and the workplace and caused a great deal of enslavement. If you are paranoid you will see this as a great conspiracy between the powerful people and the banks to enslave America.

So keep your eyes open for sycophants on the new plantation. When you identify one mentally picture an S on their forehead like Nathaniel Hawthorne's Scarlet Letter. You will find that it explains a lot that you might not understand. Suddenly everything will begin to make sense.

The new plantation came about through a large reorganization in the American economy. These were the layoffs of the 80's. It was amazing to watch. American companies, some of the largest in the world, and in America, and the richest country in the world, began laying off people by the thousands, sometimes 20,000 at a time. What was going on? It was called "downsizing" until someone came up with the more Orwellian word "rightsizing". Many people became sycophants as they struggled not to be one of the ones laid off. Good old boy networks got even tighter.

Curiously prior to that, President Reagan had been telling America about the entrepreneur. This is a word few people had ever heard. Reagan was saying that America offered great opportunities for people to become all that they could be and become rich. It was the description of a dream. Then came the layoffs, the nightmare.

Having heard Reagan's dream scenario many people were less shocked as their world collapsed around them. "I will just become one of those entrepreneurs that President Reagan is always talking about" was the thinking. I will start my own company and get rich.

Reagan's talking was almost like a set up for what he knew was coming. It seemed to be being done to soften the blow.

So Office Maxes and Office Depots spring up everywhere. "We have everything you need to become an entrepreneur" they said. Everybody was setting up small businesses and SOHOs (Small Office Home Office). Some were successful but most failed despite the incorporating, fancy letterhead and fancy business cards. Anybody can get those things but that alone does not make a successful business. The problem for most was getting that first customer.

So many entrepreneurs found themselves crawling back into the workplace, embarrassed after bragging that they were going to be rich. It is actually difficult to get back in when your resume says that for the last year or two you were self-employed. You look like a loser who failed. Companies want winners who have been getting promoted regularly for the last 15 years and not losers who got laid off and failed at their own business. Many had a hard time getting back in and fewer still received the same compensation they had when they left.

The transition to the new plantation is complete and everyone has adjusted just in time for outsourcing where, now, their jobs are being shipped off shore.

Chapter 12

The Women's Movement

"The love of liberty is the love of others. The love of power is the love of ourselves." - William Hazlitt

About this chapter I want to make it clear that I am not saying that the women's movement was (is) bad rather that it had unintended consequences. Often when we talk about the unintended consequences of a social movement, we are criticized. Social movements like the civil rights movement, women's movement and gay movement become sacred cows that we can't discuss except to talk about the goodness of the movement. But these movements have their upsides and their downsides. (And, by the way, I am pro life.)

A great change was made in America by the women's movement. Suddenly, women wanted to do men's jobs like the military, police, firemen, airline pilots, jet fighter pilots and wanted permission to kill their potential off spring if they chose to. What in the world is going on here – kill their off spring? This is just not a few crazy women. Look at the support that exists for abortion. The country is divided about half and half on this issue.

Through history and even today in the majority of the world, women have and take care of their children. What has happened to American women?

In WWII women went into the factories since the men were on the battlefield. After the war most women returned to the home. After the Civil Right's movement came the Women's Rights movement. It was as if there was a "movement industry" in place and that industry needed another job to keep itself in business. Now we have liberated the Blacks, so let's liberate the women next. It was called women's liberation as if the women were slaves.

Women, in fact, have always gotten special treatment. Men pay for the date. They are showered with gifts, flowers and candy. Doors are held open for them, heavy things are carried for them. That is a nice way to be treated. And you get to stay home from work. Is that such a bad deal?

Why would you want to drive in stop and go traffic to and from work, spend 8 hours in a stressful workplace and work for a boss who you may not like?

Suppose the roles had been reversed. Suppose that, historically, the women went off to work and the men stayed home with the kids. Suppose that historically, we sent our women into battle to die. Suppose women were bringing flowers to men constantly. There is a species of life that does that. In the lion kingdom, the female lion goes on the hunt and brings home food to the male who lays around all day. The female lion even raises the young. Perhaps the female lion says to her male off spring "don't pay attention to this stuff I am showing the girls about hunting, just watch your dad."

But if life had evolved this way regarding gender roles, what would the women think then? They would truly be slaves and in need of liberation.

The women's liberation caused many changes in American life. First, there were changes in the workplace that I have already discussed. Some are women bosses making passes at male underlings. Immediately, there were complaints about a glass ceiling and that they did not make as much money as men for the same work, Companies had to go out of their way to promote women over men to show that there was no discrimination against women. There was the first female vice president, then the first female president, then the first female CEO, then the first female policeman, then the first female firefighter, the first female airline pilot, the first female jet fighter pilot, the first female soldier in combat, the first female general, etc.

A special social class was created called "women and minorities" so that women might get the special benefits afforded to minorities and at least be counted in the statistics showing any discrimination.

Additionally, women wanted to be able to take time off from their careers to have children. Then they wanted an extended time off called maternity leave to raise them. Then they wanted to be able to return to work to the same job they left and with the same pay as if none of that had happened. If men took a year out of their career to do something, they would get a year behind in their career. Only in military service during the days of the draft, might a man expect to get his old job back at the same pay.

But the biggest effect that all this had on society was in the home. The "latch door" kids were born since both parents now worked. After school, there was no one waiting at home to give the returning kids cookies and milk. Kids began hanging out at the shopping malls.

Schools quickly became daycare centers where parents were happy just to have a place to send the kids while they were at work. Actual education became secondary, though still important. When daycare is not the issue, getting a good education is top priority for schools. When daycare is an issue, well at least we have good daycare for our tax dollars. The state began raising the children while both parents worked. Communist countries do this a lot – the state raises the children.

But this was good for the economy. Now families needed two cars and two reliable cars. We don't want mom to get stuck in traffic with a broken car. Before that there was perhaps one new car and mom had a used car to run to the market. But Detroit does not make money when someone sells a used car. Detroit wants people to buy new cars.

Two income families have more money to spend so more products are sold and the economy booms. But now the economy needs to create jobs at a faster rate since nearly twice as many people now want a job. Women vote also and we can't have a lot of unemployment among women. This was not even an issue in the 50's where the challenge was to see that all men had a job. So the government jobs machine had to crank up. The government had to create even more jobs. The good new was that women paid taxes too, so taxes available to the government grew and government grew right along with this increased revenue.

Big government was here. Latch door kids were here. A new work place was here. Declining standardized test scores were here. Troubled kids were here. But quality time was gone. It went the way of tough love as parents showered their kids with gifts to show that they loved them as a substitute for real attention.

Chapter 13

Class Warfare

"There is one law for the rich and another for the poor."
- Proverb

More and more we are hearing charges of class warfare. What is class warfare? Class warfare is not war in the traditional sense except in the case of armed revolution, like for example, the American Revolution and the French Revolution. An armed revolution is the end result of class warfare in many cases. The term, as we are hearing it used, refers to one socio-economic class taking advantage, sometimes extreme advantage, of another socio-economic class by the use of laws, policies and regulations of society's institutions. The societal institutions include more than just government and can refer to businesses such as banks.

The advantage taken usually has, as its goal, some kind of exploitation either economic or political. Slavery in the South is an example of class warfare where Blacks were kept down as a matter of law. Even after the Civil War, Blacks were kept down as a matter of law and social policy. The Civil Rights laws of the 60's, nearly 100 years after the Civil War, intended to put an end to that. It is said that the North won the war but the South won reconstruction.

So do we still have class warfare and how does it happen? Recall that I said above that society's institutions include more than just government. There is little class warfare on behalf of the government because of our court system. Since class warfare is a form of discrimination, any efforts at the government level would quickly be taken to court.

The government's role in class warfare is one of omission rather than commission. For example, suppose businesses are taking advantage of people, not just people but people belonging to a particular socio-economic class. Typically, these are poor people and typically this advantage results in transfer of wealth from one class to another. This is not the government at work but if the government allows it to happen, then the government is enjoined into the process, not by its action but by its inaction. This is an important distinction.

There are many examples of class warfare and actions to end it. For example, banks used to red line districts based on zip code. These were poorer zip code areas. The bottom line was that if you lived in one of those zip codes, you did not get the loan, period. This practice was ended by the government so that each individual person has to be evaluated separately for approval or disapproval of a loan. This was not racist since the zip code area might contain poor white people. It was the social class of being poor that was the discriminator and the discriminating party was the rich class who owned the banks. Thus class warfare.

We see this today with interest rates. If you are rich you will probably have good credit. If you are poor your credit may not be as good. So the interest rate you pay for a loan, if you are in the poor lower class, will be higher than the interest rate you will pay if you are in the rich upper class. This means that poor people will pay more for everything they buy on credit.

Banks defend this policy by saying that many poor people default on the loan and we lose money but we make up that loss by charging others in that class more for interest so that in the end we come out even. The decision is based only on one's credit score and not on accessing the individual. There are reasons for a poor credit score. Perhaps, as so often happens in today's economy, the person was laid off. He or she then missed some payments and got bad credit rating. Perhaps now they have a job and are back on their feet. Perhaps you should talk to the individual and make your decision based on your evaluation of their current situation rather than letting the computer reject them based on their credit score..

But all this takes time and costs money. It is easier to let the computer make the lending decision based on credit score alone. Such a policy discriminates against all people in the class that were laid off, missed some payments but are now back on their feet. These will generally be people in the lower economic class and thus class warfare. Here is an example where the government turns a blind eye to the problem. Bankers testify before Congress and the rich contribute to Congressional campaigns. So the government by its omission is enjoined in the class warfare and thus becomes a party to it, while the poor pay more for everything they buy on credit.

Another example is the volume discount. If you buy one of something it may cost you one dollar. If you buy ten units of that you can get them for 90 cents or a 10 percent discount. You will use ten of these over time so that would be the way to go. Except that you are poor and can't afford to buy ten. In this example, the rich who can afford to buy in volume would get 10% off everything they buy while the poor pay full price. One can argue that it should not matter how many you buy and that the unit of product is always sold at the same price to everyone who wants it. The ten units were not any cheaper to make just because they were sold in units of ten. The warehouse will still have to be restocked so there is no shelf space savings.

Now this theory does not apply to everything. Some things are cheaper if they are made in great volume due to machine setup and production run costs. But some things, like everyday products, say, tooth paste are not. The same amount is made based on purchasing forecasts. That they are sold in units or ten doesn't make the production run any cheaper. Not only that, but the guy who bought ten will not be purchasing anymore for a long time. He may have in fact cleaned our your supply, causing a future customer to be disappointed at your store because he cannot find what he wants. He then goes to another store and may continue shopping there because he can always find what he wants there.

The bottom line is that volume buying, if you can afford it, makes your purchases cheaper. The poor can't afford it and so pay more. So the upper class pays less. Some may say that this is just business and that is true but it is a practice that discriminates against a class of people.

Throughout American history class warfare was overt. During the labor movement where workers wanted to organize to get better pay and better working conditions, some people actively fought the movement. Again, during the Civil Rights movement, people actively fought against legislation to give Blacks the right to vote and equal access to credit. This was overt class warfare. Today there is more overt class warfare. Some say that there is no class warfare at all and that businessmen can have any policies they want in our free marketplace as long as the policies do not openly and directly discriminate in a way that they violate the Constitution. The argument put forth is that these people who are paying higher interest rates do not have to make the loan or get the credit card. People are free to buy whatever products they want and pay whatever price they are willing to pay. This is freedom, quickly followed by the Latin phrase "caveat emptor' (let the buyer beware).

But the argument can be made that there are people that are uneducated and can't compute interest rates and the other things that it takes to be a wise shopper. Rebuttal is that these people went to the same public schools as everyone else and other people who attended these same schools and had these same teachers learned how to become wise shoppers.

That rebuttal is not exactly fair because there are good schools and poor schools. For example, the kids who go to schools in the inner city do not get the same quality of education as the kids who go to suburban schools. The kids who go to schools in poor southern states may not get the same quality education as the kids who go to schools in wealthier states. State spending for education on a per pupil basis varies greatly from state to state. Still a public education is available to everyone and even at a bad school you can learn something if you want to. The question is do you want really to learn something?

The larger point is that for whatever reason, the poor as a class are not wise shoppers and often buy on impulse. If businessmen take advantage of this situation, then it becomes class warfare in an economic sense.

And often businessmen do take advantage of the plight of the poor. Often sales materials are misleading both about the product and its cost. Bait and switch is a good example. A thing being advertised looks like a good deal. When you get there it was misrepresented but "we do have this one" the sales line goes. "It's only a little more." Sometimes you get there and they are out of the product being advertised. Again the sale's line goes "but we do have this one which is better and just a little more expensive."

Bait and switch is illegal in most states but enforcing it is a problem .First, the victim has to report this to the state's consumer protection agency. Well right off, the poor are not likely to call a state agency. The poor are generally intimidated by the government. They can be counted on to just move on and forget it. Businessmen know that.

Bankers are famous for this house financing scheme. You are all excited just about to buy your first house. The loan is approved it is just a matter of signing the papers. This is a great day in your life. Then you get to the bank and find out about the hidden and miscellaneous fees that are to be added on. What do you do? You can refuse the loan and walk away, and end your dream of being a home owner for the first time in your life, or you can continue your dream and sign the papers. Most sign the papers. This is economic warfare against the middle class. They are not immune from class warfare. Only the upper class is immune from class warfare.

The scams go on and on while the government looks on and waits for a complaint to be filed. Then we hear how understaffed they are and how many complaints they have to process. If we hired more people, government would just get bigger and taxes would go up.

But there is, besides economic class warfare, there is political class warfare. Here there is the attempt to disenfranchise the voter from the political process where laws might be enacted to end economic class warfare. Political class warfare is harder. In the past this included poll taxes for voting which the poor could not afford. Poll taxes have been eliminated as a qualification for voting.

In recent elections the charge has been made that the ballots were too complicated for the uneducated to understand. This was the issue with the now famous "butterfly ballot" used in the 2000 Florida presidential election. Often the ballot has certain names at the top of the ballot or perhaps there is something on the back of the ballot that the voter misses. It may have been put on the back on purpose.

Sometimes the polling places are too far away for certain people to vote. Sometimes there are too few polling places resulting in long and frustrating lines in certain neighborhoods. Often people see the long line and just forget about voting.

All these things are being looked into but these are the reasons that there are claims of class warfare.

Those who complain about this real or imaginary class warfare are often accused of playing the race card. This is because those who suffer from class warfare often belong to the same race. Thus, complaining about class warfare is complaining about the mistreatment of a particular race and those who oppose any change to eliminate the class warfare are then racists. Playing the race card can be very effective as a political tactic. Those accused of racism have to scramble to clear their name. The point of the race card is to get someone to offer their support for a change just to prove that they are not a racist at all. It is political arm twisting at its finest.

The rich are able to buy support for their position with campaign contributions. The poor, having little money, cannot take this avenue. So to win, they sometimes have to play the race card.

All these racist accusations merely dilute the term causing many people to say "Yeah, I'm racist so what."

Chapter 14

The Wimpification of America.

"A coward dies a thousand deaths the brave dies but once." - Shakespeare

Wimpification? What's that? Wimpification is the process by which a people are turned into wimps. Such people are sometimes called "sheeple". This process is going on right now in America so let's discuss it. First, what is a wimp? Wimps are not manly. There is a question in the public discourse today – "Where have all the real men gone?" That only begs the question "what is a real man?"

So I will avoid offering definitions that everyone will not agree with let's just say that we all know what we are talking about here. If you are a really cute girl or pretty woman you are not going to date a wimp. Women like real men because it's a competitive world and real men compete more successfully than wimps. Real men can intimidate, wimps cannot. Ultimately, this means that they will make more money and their wife will have a bigger and better house and a bigger and better automobile and finer clothes. It's been going on this way since the beginning of mankind and goes on even in the animal kingdom. Intimidation is the most natural of behaviors. Therefore it's hard to say that it is wrong.

Becoming a man is a special part of most cultures. Usually there are rites of passage for this. In some cultures this might involve spending a week in the woods or jungle alone. In other cultures this may involve combat. Sometimes it involves circumcision. There is normally a ritual associated with entering manhood. There is usually a test to be passed. This process also goes back to the beginning of man. Manhood is a club that you have to earn your way into in many cultures.

Curiously none of this exists for womanhood or at least not nearly to the extent that it exists for becoming a man. But we men don't complain about it.

Americans have no formal process for becoming a man. Boys are expected to play and possibly excel at sports. Boys play games that involve competition and where there is a winner and a loser. Women traditionally have activities that involve cooperation like making a quilt. All these activities are to train youth of both sexes for the roles they will play as adults. Thus, girls play with dolls to prepare them for motherhood while boys play with weapons to prepare them for combat.

Part of the wimpification process is to destroy these traditional roles, called gender roles. Women now play most sport's games including, of all things, boxing. Women now work as airline pilots, jet fighter pilots, policemen, firemen and soldiers. All this is not as much a part of women's liberation as it is part of wimpification stating that there is nothing special about being a man and that women, traditionally thought of as the weaker sex, can do this too. Rather than women being brought up to the level of men, men are actually brought down to the level of women. Thus, wimpification.

Take child birth. Once the man paced back and forth across the waiting room waiting for the blessed event. Today, men assist in the delivery and cut the umbilical cord. They attend the Lamaze sessions. Child birth was once woman's work and women did it together but now men are reduced to the level of doing this women's work. Men are now airline stewardesses and nurses and women are fighter pilots.

Another great example of wimpification can be seen in TV commercials. In TV commercials today, the woman is always in charge and the man is portrayed as a bumbling idiot. This is because the wife usually makes the spending decisions so the commercials are directed towards women. Look for this. Become sensitized to this. You will see it everywhere. The problem with such commercials is that kids watch these too. Kids learn from everything they see. They come to understand the relationship between husband and wife, in part, by watching TV commercials where the wife is dominant and the husband is submissive. This programs the kids subconsciously. It's everywhere and you might not have ever noticed. So look for it.

Kids play games in elementary school during PE. When I was going to school, the girls and boys were divided up playing different games. Now they play together and more importantly the games are not competitive rather more teamwork based and they don't keep score so there are no winners and losers. It was felt that the self-esteem of the losers would suffer. Now this is all rosy but in real life which we are supposed to be preparing the kids for, there is competition and there are winners and losers. Indeed, learning how to lose is a desirable skill to have. You have to learn how to pick yourself up and do better next time. This change in elementary school PE is all part of the wimpification process. Dodge ball has been dropped in many schools because it's too violent.

The point may be that since boys and girls now play together, maybe we should take away the things that the weaker sex can't do well. Yet women do compete well in sports with other women. There are even women boxers. Soon there may be a women's football league. Picture what the tackles will look like on those teams.

Take actors of the past and present. The actors of the 40's and 50's were John Wayne, Kirk Douglas, Burt Lancaster.

These were real men as role models. Who do we have today? Well Schwarzenegger, Eastwood and Rambo fill the bill but in general, the male actors today are softer.

Then there are the messages being sent to the world that American men can't get it up without the help of drugs. TV is replete with commercials about male enhance pills. By the shear number of these commercials running constantly, one would get the idea that American men are all impotent. In all these commercials there is always the wife or girlfriend who is encouraging her man to take these drugs as if she is disappointed in him. She can do her part but he cannot. Even if those drugs had been available in the 50's, those commercials would not be allowed on TV. We were a different nation in those days. Today, it's all about sex. It's important to remember that kids see these commercials too and above the 4th grade they know what this is all about.

There are other examples of wimpification. When I was a kid we played baseball. Now kids generally play softball. We had the intimidating high dive at the swimming pool. A great rite of passage was to dive head first into the water 9 feet below. I still remember the first time I did that. Now the high dives have been removed from public pools. Many towns are removing the deep end of the pool all together. No more swimming down to the drain and touching it as a test of manhood.

I used to like to ride my motorcycle with the wind rushing through my hair. Now I have to wear a helmet. I even have to wear a helmet when I ride my bike around the neighborhood.

All this is done in the name of safety. But safety can also be called insurance company profits. I call this "insurance company legislation." It works like this. Accidents cost insurance companies money which reduces their profits. So they lobby to get laws passed to make the world safer. But these laws often take away personal freedoms like my being able to ride my bike without my helmet. Kids no longer enjoy the thrill of diving and learning to do a one & a half off the high dive. But insurance companies make more money in the process.

I do not object to making kids wear bike helmets but after age 21 you have a right to risk your life for the thrill of it. This is none of government's business. It will be difficult to convince me that the government cares if I live or die. But I understand that the insurance companies do.

So there are forces at work to make America a softer, less warlike country. It is actually a Leftist attack on American manhood. I used to be against sports in school thinking that money should be spent for education and that sports could take place out of school. I have changed my mind on this. Sports are the last place where manhood is encouraged. The coach teaches his kids the right lessons. They learn to lose and they learn to win. They learn to be tough. The coach, unlike their teachers, treats the kids like men. The coach, unlike their teachers, doesn't put up with their attitude or any whining. The coach talks to them man to man.

ROTC does the same thing. Kids learn discipline. They learn pride. Thus, there is an attack on ROTC in schools by the Left. Many want it removed all together. Military training in school? What a horrid thought. Why don't we teach them knitting and quilt making instead?

There is nothing wrong with being a man with all that implies. There is nothing wrong with teaching young males how to be a man. We cannot and should not strive for a unisex world. This is in fact acting against nature. It's acting against 10,000 years of civilization.

Chapter 15

The Softening Military

"The mounted knight is irresistible. He would bore his way through the walls of Babylon."

It all started in 1949 when the Department of War was renamed the Department of Defense. Curiously, we have not won a war since. Korea was a tie, Viet Nam was a loss, Kuwait was really the police action that the Korean War was called, the Taliban are active again in Afghanistan and Iraq is still a mess. There have been a few successful military engagements to be fair. But these were not wars, even though the Leftist press liked to refer to them as such.

Politically correct phrases like "winning the peace" and "winning the hearts and minds" have replaced phrases like "take no prisoners" as the military is softened by the politicians. On that matter I will quote the poster which Charles Colson, lawyer to President Nixon, had in his office. It read "When you have them by the balls, their hearts and minds will follow." This is the attitude that it takes to win a war.

The way things are going we are on the verge of naming the Department of Defense as the Department of Peace. I am sure we will see efforts towards that in the future. George Orwell would smile in his grave.

There are several milestones along this path of softening the military. The entire process is great news to some who would eliminate the military completely if they could. Carter cut the military back as did Clinton while Reagan built up the military. The lines are clear relative to political parties. President Obama wants to eliminate "don't ask, don't tell" so that gay soldiers and sailors can openly brag about having sex with another man. Sure, who is looking forward to taking a shower with them?

I suppose these people would just talk to the aggressors and try to make them see the right thing to do." Now come on Adolf you don't really want to invade these countries. What would the world think? Why don't you just destroy all this weaponry and live in peace with the rest of us? Would you like another cup of tea?" There are evil people out there in the world and they are not going to be reasoned with. Their goal is to destroy us, not reason with us. That is why we need a military. We have a fine military but they have to take their orders from politicians who will do and say anything to get re-elected..

So here are some milestones in the softening process. I am not discussing budget cuts by Congress, a weakening process itself, but more fundamental changes.

The first was the elimination of the draft. There was a time when all fit males went into armed services. I was an officer in the Navy. All my friends went into something. Then came the unpopular Viet Nam war. Having been told that the war was wrong, mainly by college professors and other Liberals who had access to the public, kids saw no reason to go. Marches against the war began and kids burned their draft cards. The reaction was to eliminate the draft. Democracy works.

The idea was to create a professional armed services manned by people who wanted to be there. This too sounds like a good idea until you look at the unintended consequences.

For example, everybody from my generation back can relate to the military. We were in it. To citizens today, the military is a strange place. Many think that we are in danger of the military taking us over and taking away our freedoms like happens in third world countries.

So by eliminating the draft, there is a disconnect between the military and the citizenry.

Another consequence is in the American male's perception of himself. When you go into the military you come to think of yourself as a warrior, a real man. You are proud, self confident, and self-assured. You were tested and passed the test. You hold your head high.

Entire generations of American males felt that way about themselves. This has forced the Left to change the definition of a "real man" to something that any man can claim, regardless of having military service or not. I have no particular problem with that except there has to be a name for men who risked their life in battle to protect their country. What, if not real men, are we going to call those men. I am open to suggestions.

Here is a personal story. While in California I approached a recruiter (head hunter) about getting me another job. He asked for my resume. He looked over it. Towards the top I stated that I had been a Lieutenant in the U.S. Navy. Military service is something people have put on their resume since at least World War II. It showed that I had leadership shills and personal discipline, a thing that most employers value.

The recruiter told me to take that off my resume and not to mention it during a job interview. I was astounded and asked for the reason. He explained that the person reading my resume or interviewing me probably was from the boomer generation and probably was not in the military. Indeed, he may have burned his draft card. You will come across looking like a warrior and that will subconsciously intimidate him. He will not want to have you around telling war stories to the staff. They may come to admire you more than him. Wimps do not want real men around for the same reason that fat women don't want thin women around.

I removed the reference to my military service but only after much soul searching. Is it now a negative to have served in the armed services? Those Viet Nam veterans certainly experienced that. I suspect that the Iraqi veteran will suffer the same fate.

Another milestone in the softening of the military was women in the military. There were always nurses but the new breed of woman wanted to serve in combat. This demand was safe now since had there still been a draft, the issue would switch to drafting women and putting them in combat. That would never fly.

Additionally, women wanted to attend the military academies. Special arrangements had to be made for dormitories, bath rooms and the entire academy training had to be softened. Where as you could ask a guy to hit the deck and do 50 pushups, a thing I did many times, you can't ask a woman to do that. Nor can you hit them in the gut. Nor can you run them for a mile holding their M1 rifle above their head.

The reason for disallowing combat service for women has some merit. If captured in combat, they are sure to be raped, possibly becoming pregnant with the enemy's child. Also, the thought of a woman, who we men are supposed to protect, having her head blown off in combat conjures up an awful image. There just seems to be something fundamentally wrong with having some kid's mother dying in combat to defend our country. This is the women's movement gone mad. Remember if you are on the battlefield even in the rear, you could find yourself in combat at any moment.

So now the great country of America is defended, in part, by its women. I don't think that we are so desperate for warriors to have to do that. It has the effect of saying that there is nothing special about men. Women can do this too.

Following close on the heels of that in milestones are gays in the military. I would feel uncomfortable taking a shower with a gay man looking at my genitals.

There was a "don't ask don't tell" policy initiated by President Clinton but that has come under attack now. Gays think that it is somehow discriminatory that they cannot proudly announce that they are gay. I personally have a problem being given an order to go into battle and possibly get killed by a man who goes to bed with and has sex with another man. I would find it hard to respect such a man and take orders from him. I would go into battle with him but not want to be sent into battle by him.

Gays in the military, implemented by boomer President Clinton, who never served in the military himself, have caused a big morale problem for the services. Of course, like women, gays will demand to go into combat as well and given the seniority nature of promotions in the service, soon a gay man will be ordering heterosexual men into battle to die. Soon there will be gay generals ordering battalions of men into battle.

The softening of the military includes the training changes made when the soldiers were volunteers and not draftees. You can do anything to a draftee, he is stuck there. When word gets out how the volunteers are being treated if the same rough training is kept, there would quickly be a drop in volunteers. Few would want to go through what we went through. I took my training under a Marine drill sergeant. I hit the deck to do 50 pushups many times.

The tough training has a purpose. It's to turn boys into men. Battle is not only physically challenging its mentally challenging. It's easy to get scared and hide behind a tree.

What you need is nerve. What you need is courage. That is the purpose of military training. You have to come to feel that if you can survive that, you can survive anything. The rougher the training, the more you will come to feel that. The easier the training, the less you will come to fell that you can survive anything.

Here is a personal story about my training. A cadet in the class above us tried to kill himself by slitting his wrists. Word quickly spread through the ranks about this. We were called into formation. The drill sergeant said "I suppose you have all heard about the cadet who tried to kill himself." I was thinking "Here we go. Now we are going to get the lecture that this is only training and if you are really having trouble, there are people you can talk to. Don't take this too seriously, etc." Instead, the drill sergeant said "Do any of you son of a bitches want to take the easy way out? If so, let me know and I will buy you the razor blades." Then we ran for 3 miles. That is when I realized that this was some serious business.

Now I want to make it perfectly clear that we have some fine, brave soldiers in the military today. I do not want to denigrate these men. What I am talking about are trends, trends that add up to a softening military.

If not already, soon there will come a call to eliminate religion from the military. In the case of religion in the military, we are talking about spending tax payer's dollars for government support of religion. If that is not a violation of the doctrine of separation of church and state, I don't know what is.

So how will this play out. Tax dollars being spent to pay the salaries of men of the cloth. Tax dollars being spent to make these pastors, priests and rabbis available to soldiers. How about the churches that exist on military bases? Those churches cost tax dollars to build and maintain. Will the military be forced to perform same sex marriages in churches on military bases and by military chaplains? This is coming. Will the two men be able to give each other a big sloppy wet kiss after the ceremony like non same sex couples do and while dressed in full military uniform? This too is coming.

This hasn't come under attack yet because the other side has to move slowly. You can't ask for everything at once. First get gays in. They demand that they do not have to keep their orientation a secret. Then demand that they are allowed in combat giving orders to heterosexual men. Then you can press for gay marriages in military churches. Everything in its time.

So there is a clear discernable trend in place. The common ingredient in all these activities underway is a softer military. We are losing the big stick that we are supposed to be carrying while speaking softly. Compare this with the lack of political will daily expressed in Congress and our enemies will come to think that we are soft and even if we had the will to fight, our military may be too soft to fight. This happened to the Romans.

There is actually a very good argument to having a draft. There will be fewer wars if we have a draft. Why? With a professional military the thinking is that these people volunteered for this and in that sense they asked for it. This is what they are getting paid to do. To their parents and loved ones I would point out that they asked for this and knew that at any time they could be sent to war.

Now compare that to a draft system. These people did not ask to go into battle, they did not volunteer for this. Their parents will say that I don't want my kid killed in this war which I don't understand the need for in the first place.

In such a system, there would be tremendous pressure placed on Congress not to approve funding for wars. There would have to be a very good justification to go to war. America or at least our critical interests would have to be threatened with no other recourse but to go to war. All other avenues would have to be exhausted.

We would have never had the Iraqi war had we still had a draft. But we would have had the war in Afghanistan, the get even war, because the people who attacked us on 9/11 were trained in Afghanistan.

Then there is the policy of "don't fire until fired upon." The problem with that thinking is that he may kill you with his first shot. Then your buddy can fire back I suppose. Our enemies know that this is our policy. Kind and gentle to be sure but it is not the way to win a war or to defend a nation. In the Iraqi war the first rule we should have made and announced to the world is that we are going to shoot, on the spot, any male we see with a rag covering his face. We see them on CNN dancing in the streets, waving their rifles and with their faces covered. How are we going to identify them?

So now we have generals out trying to win the peace and trying to win the hearts and minds of the people and women and homosexuals in combat. They are at least on the battle field. When on the battle field, you can find yourself in combat at any moment.

Another issue is the definition of torture. What can you do to a captured terrorist to get him to talk. There is physical torture and mental torture. Physical torture has generally been outlawed for a long time. But now the attack is on mental torture. It seems that that shouldn't be allowed either. While physical torture is easy to define, mental torture is not. Mental torture is in the mind of the one being tortured. Some would say that simple solitary confinement for an extended period of time is mental torture. Some would say that intimidation is mental torture. Some would say that threats are mental torture. Some would say that sleep deprivation is mental torture. Soon we will be required to give captives their Miranda rights on the battle field. Intelligence is key to winning a war and we need to find out what the captured soldier knows. It saves American soldier's lives. So we seem to prefer to risk the lives of our soldiers rather than mentally torture the enemy. Is that soft or what?

An issue that has arisen today concerns the quality of our military. This is just another attack on the military, in general, but some say that the military is full of losers. The notion is that those who go into the volunteer military have no other life options like, say, college. We are to believe that the stupid go into the military. The facts do not bear this out since there are qualifications that must be met to go into the military. All this is meant to discredit the military in general. So now, instead of the military attacking the enemy, we have the Liberals attacking the military.

Today's military has been changed by technology. No longer do you have to cut off a man's head face to face. Now you push a button which launches a cruise missile and perhaps a hundred people are killed. You never see them or hear them cry out in pain. But, is interesting to note that the Muslim terrorists do just that. They cut off people's heads, film it and put it on the Internet. That is what terrorism is all about – terror. The weak back down in the face of it. The Spanish pulled out their troops after the first train bombing in Madrid. The point is to make you too scared to fight. Terrorism works.

In fact, we have a fine military with brave men and women defending our country. But how long this will last is debatable.

Chapter 16

Why Racism is Alive and Well and the Race Card

"Civil Right's leaders have 52 cards in their deck also - the ace of spades and 51 race cards." - Bill Pirkle

This is a brief overview of the civil rights movement past and present. Even though I am not black I know something about this. I was born and grew up in Atlanta, Georgia. I clearly remember water fountains marked white and colored as were the restrooms. I clearly remember the sign on the bus that read "colored seat from the rear." I lived through this albeit as a white person.

Was it racist? No, to us that was the way it was. We did not think that we were doing anything wrong. There was national government sanctioned segregation. It was built into state laws, regulations and policies. Who started the policy of integration in America? It was Republican President Eisenhower. He integrated the military setting the stage for other things to be integrated. Kennedy actually started the Civil Rights movement and this was completed by President Johnson.

The aim was to end government sanctioned segregation. After a number of laws were passed, Blacks could sit anywhere, use any water fountain, use any restroom, vote, get credit and be considered equally when applying for a job or renting an apartment or buying a house. This, of course, applies not only to Blacks but to any minority, those who are now referred to as people of color. There is absolutely no government sanctioned segregation in America today.

But is there still racism? Well, there is no government sanctioned racism but there may be personal racism. Some people may not like Blacks or other people of color. Personal racism goes by another name – personal freedom. The government can't pass a law saying who you cannot like. It's one of your basic rights to like or not like someone and for whatever reason you choose. Maybe you don't like their skin color, maybe you don't like their manners, maybe I don't like the way they wear their hair. We are free to not like anyone for any reason we chose to give. It is a basic freedom that everyone enjoys.

But say in this nation of 300 million people, that 100 million exercise the personal freedom to not like Blacks. That's nearly a third of the nation. Now is that racism? Well, it's a form of collective racism but its not government sanctioned racism as the term is being used here, moreover it's perfectly legal.

It's doubtful if the number is as high as 100 million but there maybe a significant number of people who do not like minorities of any color. Indeed, there may be a significant number of minorities that do not like white people. (We are called "whitie" after all. Why isn't that called the "W word" and forbidden like the N word?) This is divisive but not illegal. Whether or not it is immoral is a question for the philosophers to answer.

Let's assume that this is the case. Then is there racism in America? The answer would have to be yes but it is a personal racism and not a government sanctioned racism.

Then it would be reasonable to ask why is there personal racism? I think even with personal racism there are few people who dislike all of a particular minority sect. Most might dislike some minorities or even most minorities. Who could not like Diana Ross or Denzel Washington?

So now we are led to asking the question "why do many people not like many minorities?"

This is where it gets complicated. There are probably different reasons for different minority groups and even sub-groups within minority groups. For example, take black kids who write rap music. Their lyrics routinely call women bitches and whores. I can understand why someone might not like them and by extension people who like that music. Since 70% of babies born in the ghettos are illegitimate I can think of reasons that some may not like these girls and women.

How about white businessmen who cheat minorities by taking advantage of their lack of understanding of the marketplace. I can see why minorities would not like these white businessmen and by extension whites in general.

So it becomes clear that what people are not liking is not physical bodies of a particular color but the behavior or those bodies. So the reasoning goes like this. I do not like certain behaviors. Most of the people in this particular minority sect exhibit those behaviors. Therefore, I do not like those minorities. Is that racism? Well, yes, but it not derived at directly based on race rather indirectly based on behavior.

It there anything wrong with not liking certain behaviors? I don't think so. And it's not my fault that those behaviors can be associated with people in a certain minority group.

But this leads to another issue. Behavior is culture based. That is to say that what is improper behavior in one culture may be perfectly acceptable behavior in another culture. So the question becomes can one not like certain cultures? This is going to become the next big issue in America as we become a multi-ethnic society. We are no longer a melting pot where people blend in. People today want to maintain their own cultural heritage. This goes as far as expecting that their language is respected by government. In San Francisco's China Town, the street signs are in Chinese.

So now we have a dilemma. If the particular behavior is disliked by a great number of people but some culture accepts this behavior as appropriate, then we are actually disliking a culture and if that culture can be associated with a particular minority group or race, is this racism?

So when we ask is racism alive we first have to define racism more precisely.

I will define racism here as not liking, and therefore not wanting to associate with, people who are in a minority class and because of the way they behave. By this definition, the fact that their culture accepts this behavior is beside the point.

We can cite many cultures in the past and in the present whose culture based behaviors we would find totally unacceptable. Take female circumcision in African countries. Or the way women are treated in the Middle East. In every case their defense will be that this is our culture. Slavery was part of the culture in the South but that justification was not acceptable. Capital punishment is part of the culture in America and Europe finds it deplorable.

So eventually it is going to come down to do people have the right to have a culture that others find deplorable and is disliking that culture, and by extension those people, a form of racism?

I am using the word dislike here but I could use the word hate. Rereading this chapter and substituting the emotionally charged word hate for the more polite word dislike would bring the point home more solidly. Suddenly, we are hating behaviors, hating cultures and hating people who practice this.

Hate is really what we are talking about when all is said and done. Do we have the right to hate something?

When the civil rights movement began it quickly became highly organized. It in fact turned into an industry employing thousands of lawyers and other professions. There was a lot of hate on both sides because a culture was being changed. Cultures do not like to change. People do not like to change and certainly people do not like to see their culture change. Death is always involved when changing a culture. This is because they would rather die than live in the new culture.

During the civil rights movement which was going along nicely or at least as nicely as these things can go, a strange thing happened. Suddenly the Blacks who were well on their way to being at last a legal part of American society decided that they wanted to be separate and the Black Separatist Movement was born. Whites were confused. Wait a minute you were separate, you were segregated, and all this is to make you a part of American society, so now what is this black separatist movement all about?

Well apparently Blacks were afraid that they would lose their identity in the process and this is a fear many minority groups have today, expecting, for example, that their kids can be taught in Spanish in school. Blacks began dressing in African dress, naming their children with African names and there was once a movement to declare Black English, which many consider merely poor grammar, as a dialect of English. Ebonics was born. Then there was pressure to teach Ebonics in school. If you object you are being racist.

Being called a racist in America today has become a weapon and perhaps a sport. If you complain about crack in the ghetto you are a racist. If you hate rap music you are a racist. There is never a day goes by that somebody is not being called a racist, especially news commentators and other writers.

Politicians have to write everything down, read it, have somebody else read it before they say it to make sure that it doesn't sound racist. For a start, any criticism of any black behavior is considered racism. The Jews play this game also. Any criticism of Israel is considered anti-Semitic. Soon the other minority groups will pick up on this. Criticize Mexico for its corruption and you will be labeled anti-Hispanic. Criticize China and you will be labeled anti-Asian.

As America becomes fragmented into minority groups as in non-white, we will not be able to criticize anything for fear of offending someone and being called a racist.

The minority groups do themselves a disservice by using this word so haphazardly. The word should be reserved for real racists. As it gets overuses it gets cheapened. When everyone is a racist, no one is a racist.

Whether or not racism is alive today or just dislike for behaviors and cultures, one thing is certain, people are being routinely labeled as racists and the civil rights industry is certainly alive and well.

One may ask why do we need a civil right industry 50 years after a successful civil rights movement? The first answer that will be given is so that we never return to those days again. This is a reasonable answer since it is certainly possible if minorities drop their guard. Another answer is that it employs thousands of people who might be jobless without a civil rights industry to employ them, people like Jessie Jackson and Al Sharpton.

But there is such an industry and like all industries it wants to survive and grow. Labeling everyone a racist gives the impression that racism is alive and therefore we need the civil rights industry. Therefore, and not to sound too cynical, the civil rights industry is probably behind the racist labeling since it is in their interest that it continue and people usually do what is in their interest.

But sometimes there are self-fulfilling prophesies. Keep this going long enough and there will be racism. As more and more people talk about war, soon there is a war. Even those with patience and common sense reach a breaking point where they have had enough. Even reasonable people can get frustrated.

Among many white people today there is this frustration. First, a civil rights movement. Then billions and billions of tax dollars pumped into the black community in the form of social assistance. Special set aside contracts for minorities and hiring quotas. Where has this gotten us? Ghettos where crack is everywhere. Seventy percent of ghetto births illegitimate. Black high school dropout rate well over 60%. Black youth unemployment at 40%. Many Black fathers abandoning their children. Black gangs roaming the ghettos fighting drug wars.

Even the most patient and reasonable white can get frustrated after a while. Even Rosa Parks, the mother of the civil rights movement, the brave woman who refused to give up her seat on the bus to a white man and started all this, had her home invaded by a black gang where she was harassed and robbed. All along she told the kids "don't you know who I am, I'm Rosa Parks". Of course these kids did not know who she was. To them she was prey.

The problem is that when Dr. Martin Luther King, Jr. was assassinated, nobody of the same caliber took his place. I can not avoid saying at this point that Jessie Jackson and Al Sharpton, reverends though they may be, are not of that caliber. They are part of the civil rights machine to be sure, and making a lot of money in that industry to be sure, but as the lyric from the Credence Clearwater Revival song goes "who'll stop the rain?"

The Blacks are in fact leaderless and that is why the problems of the ghettos continue. No amount of talking, alone, will solve those problems and no amount of patience and reasonableness will prevent white frustration over this sad state of affairs.

A black friend mine, while we were discussing this, made a remarkable point. He said "why to we need a national leader?" The Chinese in America don't have a national leader, the Hispanics in America don't have a national leader, why do we need a national leader? That is a very good point for which I have no answer. There are to be sure many successful Blacks who could and do exercise some leadership. Oprah Winfrey, and Michael Jordon come quickly to mind. There are a plethora of successful Blacks in the business, sports and entertainment industries that could act as role models for black youth. But to be a role model you have to go into the ghetto and go on a regular basis.

It's fair to say that not only have whites turned their backs on the black community. successful Blacks have turned heir backs on the black community.

Here is an antidote. I was teaching and having lunch in the teacher's lounge. A black teacher began commenting that he read about a jazz contest for school aged kids in New York City. He observed that the band that won the contest did not have any Blacks in the band which disappointed him since jazz is a black invented art form. His tone insinuated that there may have been some racism at work. I normally remained quiet in situations with teachers because I have very strong feelings about what is wrong with education today and am sure to get into an argument. But that was too much for me. I can guarantee you that in music competitions the best musicians will make the cut regardless of skin color. I spoke up. I said "do you want to know why there were no Black kids in that jazz band? Because all the black kids are out shooting basketball instead of being at home practicing their instruments."

Well he thought that that was a racist remark and of course, he was offended. Well, of course, being offended today is a national sport. Everybody in the minority sects are offended by everything.

I continued "do you actually think that there was a black kid in that school that could outplay everyone else and they did not put him in the band? Why would they do that? They are trying to win the competition." The fact is what I said. Fewer black kids play musical instruments today and they spend every spare minute playing basketball. If they spent every spare minute playing their musical instruments, the entire jazz band would have been black in exactly the same way and for the same reasons that basketball teams are mostly black these days.

Property values even in the inner city neighborhoods are high. Basketball courts have the most players per square foot. Thus black inner city neighborhoods have basketball courts rather than, say, tennis courts. Thus, the great basketball players are black because they have been playing the game since they were 6 years old. If inner cities had tennis courts, all the great tennis players would be black. There is no racism involved.

Blacks have a long history of being accepted in music. Jazz and blues were music art forms invented by the Blacks. The 50's had an abundance of black singing groups. In the 60's Motown produced fine music enjoyed all over the world. The 5th Dimension, too, were world famous? Nobody is discriminating against black music except perhaps rap music whose lyrics turn a lot of people off.

I can accept rap or hip hop music as an art form but it cannot be compared with what has gone before, at least musically speaking. Perhaps it will evolve into great music in the musical sense.

So racism is alive because there are people in whose financial interest it is to keep it alive.

Chapter 17

Foreign Policy

*"No country can be trusted beyond its own self-interests"
- George Washington*

Foreign policy is the policy made by one country to deal with other countries. Relationships with countries include trade relationships, military relationships and cultural relationships to name a few. Trade relationships are the most important today, replacing the military relationships of the past which still exists but trade relations, in these days of the global economy, are paramount.

One doctrine that guides foreign policy is the idea that nations are sovereign and have a right to run themselves independent of outside interference. Specifically, it is understood and agreed to, that one country should not meddle in the internal affairs of another country. It's called sovereignty. Thus, there are dictators who regularly persecute their citizens while the world looks on.

But the practical side of foreign policy includes the notion of one country protecting their interests. Safety is a paramount interest in this regard. For example, suppose an unstable government begins developing nuclear weapons. Another country might think that stopping this is in their national interest and that might mean meddling in another country's internal affairs.

Suppose one country gets a mineral that is critical to our economy and there is a threat that this mineral might be cut off. This will cause economic problems and possibly unemployment and so this becomes something that affects their national interest.

So the practical side of foreign policy often requires one country to meddle in the internal affairs of another.

One of the truest things ever said about America's foreign policy was said by Lenin. He said "When we get ready to hang the capitalist, he will sell us the rope". In a previous chapter I said that it's all about creating jobs. Having everybody employed keeps politicians in office. Therefore, our foreign policy is all about business.

Say there is an internal conflict in a foreign country – women being raped and killed, children being killed, entire villages being destroyed. We've seen this on TV before. So what do we do? Well first we ask these questions 1) are we doing business with that country?, 2) are there any American resources immediately at risk?, 3) is this having any effects on the American economy?, 4) are American jobs at risk?, 5) is this costing America's rich any money?

If the answer to these questions is no then we say "those poor people, we have got to get the U.N. involved to stop this. We can't get involved because this is a sovereign country and we can't meddle in their internal affairs".

If the answers to at least one of these questions is "yes" then it becomes an matter of national security. We will have to get involved to protect our national interests and national security. If what is happening in Darfur was happening in Saudi Arabia, we would send troops because that is where we get our oil. That is the ultimate reason that we are fighting wars in the Middle East.

So America's foreign policy becomes very predictable for our opponents in the world. They know exactly how we will respond. They know how to play it so that we will never get involved.

America has never been particularly good at foreign policy and we are no better at it today. Take China. We need China to put pressure on North Korea to stop their nuclear program. But we can't put too much pressure on China because they hold a lot of our foreign debt with their purchase of our government securities. This supports the spending here to make everything OK for the voter, thus keeping the current politicians in power. Thus, we need China to buy our debt with their surplus of dollars, thanks to the trade deficit, thus, we can got too rough with them in foreign policy. Nor can we reveal this situation to the American people.

Viet Nam foreign policy was a total disaster. Ho Chi Min actually came to us first for help in uniting his country. The influence of the French caused us to reject him so he went to the communists. These are the same French who lobbied against us in the UN visa vi Iraq.

In recent history, Panama came to us wanting control of the Panama Canal. When we rebuffed them they reminded us that it would be impossible for us to defend it. President Carter quickly gave in and turned it over to them. This sent a message to the world that America was weak and all you had to do was threaten us. This was in 1977. Two years later in 1979, Iranian students, sensing our weakness under President Carter, took over our embassy there. They held our people hostage or over a year, 444 days, until President Reagan was elected. They sensed that he was no one to fool around with and released the hostages. The Panama Canal turnover, under veiled threat, sent the message that we were weak and now we are being pushed around by Venezuela. Little more than a third world country, they are challenging the most power country in the world.

Our foreign policy with Mexico is no better. Being invaded with illegal immigrants Mexico is protesting any efforts we have made to put up a wall at the border. The government of Mexico actually prints and hands out documents to show its citizens how to make it across the border. How "in your face" is that? What do we do? NAFTA – good for business.

Our support for Israel is the cause of most of the problems we have in the Middle East. All efforts to make peace there have failed because we won't put pressure on Israel.

President Reagan's military build up in the 80's ended the cold war. Then we were forced to lend Russia billions of dollars or, as they made the veiled threat, we can't guarantee that we can keep our nuclear weapons secure. Those billions went down a black hole and now we have Putin as the leader there. Putin, former communist and head of the intelligence organization, KGB, is now threatening the progress made toward democracy and frequently vetoing our efforts in the UN while supporting those who we are fighting. Why didn't we make our financial aid dependent on their future cooperation?

Iraq and Afghanistan is the latest example of a disastrous foreign policy. We are simply not good at foreign policy. For us it's all about money.

One dimension of our foreign policy is particularly troublesome. More and more in our trade agreements and contracts other countries are insisting in an exchange of technology as part of the deal. This is a dangerous road to go down. Technology is developed at great expense and is often a national secret. It is our advantage.

Once you start this with one country, then every country wants it as part of the deal. If you don't give it to them after having given it to others, discrimination is claimed. The country claiming discrimination has an abundance of their people in our country as immigrants thanks to our multicultural society. Many of these immigrants still have an allegiance to their homeland. Elections these days are very close so no politician wants to alienate the immigrant voters. They will put pressure on to release the technology. With the technology and the cheap labor which attracted us to them in the first place, they are in a position to compete with us later.

So we are running up a large national debt and making ourselves dependent on foreign countries who will buy it, running trade deficits with everyone we trade with, cheapening our currency, transferring valuable technology to those who might one day be our enemy and allowing their citizens to come here to be able to put pressure on our government.

And this is what we call foreign policy.

Chapter 18

The United Nations

"If the United Nations is a country unto itself, then the commodity it exports the most is words" - Ester Fein

What a great idea. We just get all the countries of the world together and they solve all the world's problems. This idea overlooks something fundamental. Nations are sovereign and they do what is in their best interests. Sometimes it may be in their best interest to support someone or something that others might actually see as part of the problem.

The United Nations was formed after WWII as a way to keep peace in the world. But then the League of Nations was formed as a way to keep peace in the world and we had WWII.

The first test for the United Nations was the Korean war. The North, North of the 38th parallel, was controlled by the communists and invaded the South, South of the 38th parallel. Under United Nations authority, the Korean War began and America sent the majority of troops. When the war ended, the communists were still North of the 38th parallel and the South was South of the 38th parallel. North Korea tried to invade the South and lost. So in the end nothing happened to North Korea. So what was the point of the war. Why did all those people die? This is typical United Nations behavior. This was their first test and the failed it.

The fact is that the United Nations is not having any more success than the League of Nations in keeping world peace. But to be fair they do do some good particularly with their agencies. They do operate the World Health Organization.

The UN is broken up into 2 bodies – the Security Council and the General Assembly. The Security Council has 5 permanent members – the United States, China, France, Russia and the United Kingdom (Britain). These members have veto power over the resolutions that are passed and resolutions are the primary way that the UN has any influence. Through resolutions, it expresses world opinion. You are better of having world opinion on your side if you can. Today, France's chief claim to fame is that she is a permanent member of the Security Council and has veto power. Were it not for that there would be little to distinguish France from South American countries.

There are ten temporary members of the Security Council which rotate among other member countries in the General Assembly. The General Assembly votes on resolutions brought forth by member states. Resolutions can vary from condemning Israel for something it has done to designating a special world holiday.

The UN is considered ineffective at establishing peace. UN peace keeping forces have actually stood by while people were being killed in front of them, having been given orders not to get involved unless attacked. The bad guys know that this is their policy so the word goes out, whatever you do don't fire on the United Nation's soldiers. Just let them watch the carnage.

But it does do some good work and it probably worth having around as long as too much is not expected of them. But lately, the trend is to take everything before the UN. Indeed some Americans think that we should not go to war without first getting UN approval. Other Americans think that we should protect our national interests and ignore the UN.

The problem with the UN on a practical basis is the assumption that they can solve international conflicts and thus these things should be taken before the UN for resolution. The problem with that thinking is that time drags on and on. With no resolution from the UN and as this time passes, things in the conflict just get worse, all the while with people thinking the something in being done. This represents a false hope that many put their faith in, especially the Left.

What the UN actually represents is a giant trading bazaar. If America wants support from other countries for a particular resolution there is a price to pay for getting this support. Perhaps countries want most favored trading status, or a loan from the World Bank or for an American corporation to set up a factory in their country to create jobs. This is often the price of political support. Curiously, it is in the interest of these countries who want things for there to be conflicts in the world so that there will be resolutions requiring their support.

Few resolutions are passed just on the rightness and wrongness of the resolution. Money always changes hands.

The veto power is often used by the 5 permanent members. During the cold war, Russia vetoed many resolutions sponsored by the United States. There too there is often a price for support but not a tacky and obvious as financial dealings on a short term scale. There the view is on strategic and long term issues.

Some think that the UN represents some sort of world government that might have control over the United States. There is little chance of that as long as we have veto power on the Security Council. The greater danger is that idea that the United States would need the approval of the UN before entering into any military action. Do we need their permission to go to war? As I said, it is true that you are better off having world opinion on your side than to not. But the UN is a place to stall things. Things can take years to finally resolve if they are ever resolved. So if we needed the UN's permission to go to war, we could spend years getting it as things worsened. For example, by the time we had the UN's permission to attack Iran, they could already have nuclear weapons. The same is true for North Korea. I am not advocating these attacks but we do not know what the future holds. It is certainly in our interest to keep nuclear weapons out of the hands of those who might want to smuggle a dirty bomb into America.

What many thought would be the death blow for the UN was the recent oil for food scandals. There the UN showed itself to be, not only corrupt, but weak in managing its own internal affairs. Yet nothing happened.

Chapter 19

The Healthcare System

"You medical people will have more lives to answer for in the other world than even we generals" - Napoleon Bonaparte

Much is being said today about America's healthcare system, There is division of course. One side says that we have the best healthcare system in the world. That may be true but everybody does not get to participate in it. The rebuke for this thinking is that if these lazy people got a job they would have healthcare also. The truth is that 40% of the uninsured work full time. They just don't work for companies that offer healthcare insurance as a benefit.

In effect we have two healthcare systems. Those who work for governments and big companies have great health care and those who work for small companies do not. (Remember the chapter on the two Americas?) Also, we hear that small businesses are creating all the new jobs, yet they can't offer healthcare insurance in many cases. This gives the big corporations a big advantage when recruiting employees over the smaller, leaner and often more efficient small businesses who compete with them for business.

To be fair, all Americans have healthcare. Those without insurance can always go to the emergency room. The problem with that is that it is extremely expensive. But the good news is that the poor can skip out on the bill. The hospital will adjust their accounting, raise their rates, and the insurance companies can pay for it with increased rates for everyone else.

The bad news is that those with some money can't do that and it might affect their credit and if there is money, the hospital may be able to get at it. You could have a heart attack or stroke and lose everything you spent your live building up.

Essentially, there is one healthcare system for the rich and one system for the poor. For some reason that is not totally unexpected. It works like airline seats.

There have been efforts to reform our healthcare system it is always met with the same reaction. Do we want the same poor healthcare system as England or Canada has? This fits in with the idea that we have the best healthcare system in the world.

This idea is hard to swallow. Am I to understand that the people of Europe, Japan, Australia and Korea are getting substandard healthcare? These societies have been around for a thousand years. The people of Germany are getting substandard healthcare? That is hard to believe. These countries have prosperous economies. Many of their citizens are wealthy.

So apparently we are to believe that our two tier, rich/poor, healthcare system is superior to all the healthcare systems in the civilized world. This is hard to accept.

There are several reasons for our two tier system. Primarily it's the cost of healthcare that is the root of the problem. There was a time when nearly all companies offered healthcare to their employees. So what went wrong? Why are costs so high these days?

First, we are getting different healthcare, more high tech healthcare. For example, there were no CAT scans in the old days. Many of today's blood tests were not available. Many of today's drugs were not available. To that extent, we do have great, high tech healthcare but the rest of the world has access to all this technology too. But this technology makes healthcare more expensive than it used to be.

Secondly, there is the lawyer angle. We create thousands of lawyers a year. These lawyers need money. As a lawyer they have three choices. They can work for federal, state and local governments as prosecutors or they can go into practice for themselves as defense attorneys or they can work for corporations as corporate lawyers. Most take the private practice route since there are a limited number of jobs working for governments and corporations.

Besides divorces, wills etc. many private practice lawyers get involved in suing someone on behalf of their clients. It seems that everybody is suing everybody these days. This is actually a good thing. This makes us safe. There are a plethora of lawyers, sitting like vultures on a power line just waiting for someone to make a mistake. Businesses know this. So they are very careful. This makes us safe when we buy food or buy anything.

But they also sue doctors for malpractice. This causes doctors to have to carry malpractice insurance. Doctors can pay $400,000 and more a year for malpractice insurance. These costs are passed on to the patient and then to the healthcare insurance companies who have to raise their rates for healthcare insurance. Small companies can't afford these rates so many workers do not have healthcare insurance.

Lawyers have a good defense for their behavior. They say that doctors are different today. They are now incorporated and their offices run like assembly lines to maximize throughput. First, the nurse comes in and takes your temperature and weight. The nurse does a little paperwork and leaves. Then the doctor, running from treatment room to treatment room, often spending no more than 10 minutes with the patient. They can process 100 or more patients a day often at $100 or more per office visit. That's $10,000 per day in income.

Lawyers argue that when a doctor works that fast and sees that many patients, the doctor is bound to make mistakes. When they make a mistake, like failing to catch something in a diagnosis, or misdiagnosing an illness or perhaps prescribing the wrong medication, we are there to sue him/her. That is a valid point. There have been cases in operating rooms where the patient was sewn up with an instrument still inside them. There have been people diagnosed with a cold when they had pneumonia. There have been people diagnosed with stomach flu when they had stomach cancer. There are many horror stories in the best healthcare system in the world.

So lawyers will argue that they protect the public against "assembly line" doctors who are out to make as much money as possible.

But they really don't protect the public that much. The doctor just gets malpractice insurance and passes the cost along to the insurance companies. What would protect the public would be if the doctor could not get malpractice insurance. Then the doctor would have to be careful.

So rising healthcare costs put it out of the reach of many including those employed by small companies.

But now we have Obabmacare. It has some good features. First, it stops health insurance from cherry picking those they will insure, minimizing their risk and maximizing their profits. Insurance by its very nature is taking risk where they lose in some cases and win in other cases and then setting the rates accordingly to make a profit.

Obamacare stops this cherry picking by prohibiting health insurance companies from refusing insurance because of pre-existing conditions. The problem with that is that people will go without insurance until they get sick. Then they will buy insurance (with the pre-existing condition.) Now the insurance company will have to take them and just pass the costs on to the other policy holders. Thus everybody's rates will go up.

Another problem for Obamacare is the requirement that everyone buy health insurance. This will be tested in the courts. The Constitution allows Congress to "regulate" commerce. The question is can the government force someone to buy something like healthcare insurance if they don't want it. Is that regulating commerce? It's doubtful if the Supreme Court will agree so that part may be dropped.

But then since the whole purpose of this in the first place was to get insurance for everyone and since the so called public option was dropped under political pressure, then when the smoke settles, everyone will not have insurance. So what was the point?

The point became to give Obama a victory.

Then the problem is how will the current system absorb another 30 million people if they can somehow get insurance. Waiting lines will get longer for everybody.

This should have been done one step at a time and not in one encompassing law.

What they failed to address, and this would have lowered costs and cost nothing, was tort reform and interstate sales of healthcare insurance. Recall that the trail lawyers are a big contributor to the Democratic party and they do not want tort reform They make millions suing doctors. This forces doctors to practice defensive medicine by ordering tests that may be unnecessary which raises everyone's cost. But then lawyers cannot argue that the doctor should have ordered this or that test. Doctors just order all the tests that might possibly apply to the patient's ailment. It's called "defensive medicine" and runs up everyone's costs.

As far as interstate purchasing of health insurance, the issue is this. State insurance commissioner, elected officials, must approve a company that sells insurance in their state. Many states have only approved a few companies which limits competition and keeps prices high. So why not allow every company to sell in the state or allow the public to buy from companies doing business in another state? We can buy car insurance that way.

There is no good answer to this question. Naturally, the companies would be against this since it would increase their competition. Insurance commissioners would be against this as well since it would lessen their power to select which companies their public can choose from. Probably a lot of money in the form of campaign contributions changes hands in that decision process.

When they get serious about lowering the price of health insurance, they will consider tort reform and interstate purchasing of health insurance. Until then, the Congress does not look sincere about solving this national problem.

Chapter 20

Raising Children Today

"You can do anything with children if you will only play with them." - Prince Otto von Bismark

Like everything else in America today, raising children has changed. Raising children is a cultural issue and so when the culture changes, how children are raised changes.

In my day children were raised to be polite and respect adults. We said "yes ma'am" and "No ma'am" and "yes sir" and "no sir" to our teachers and parents in most cases. We sat quietly at the table and the watchword was "don't speak until spoken to". We had a weekly allowance which was earned by doing predetermined chores around the house. Chores included cutting the grass. We were expected to keep our room tidy.

When we got into trouble at school there was a note from the teacher or principal that had to be signed and returned to school the next day. Getting that note signed always involved a lecture about how embarrassing this is to us, the parents. There was usually a spanking or switching involved. We had to go into the yard and cut the switch and knew what would happen if the switch was too small. (a switch is a small branch of a bush whose leaves are removed and is used on the bare legs. It stings like the devil and usually brings to the eyes.

We all were in the Boy Scouts and regularly went on weekend camping trips in the summer. There we learned how to pitch a tent, build a safe fire, often started with a flint or magnifying glass. We cooked meals and washed the dishes. We dug the latrine and filled it back in when the tents came down.

During the day we played games like fox and the hounds, went on field trips looking for certain bugs, identified plants and watched out for snakes. Given the push towards environmentalism today, it's surprising that there is not more interest in getting kids out into the woods on camping trips.

My toys were erector sets with which I built things, a telescope where I looked at the stars and the planets, a microscope where saw all that stuff in my drinking water. I looked at everything I could get my hands on through my microscope. And guns, lots and lots of guns. I always got cowboy guns for Christmas and my friends and I killed each other many times over. We knew that is was play and there was little violence in society in the 50's.

It was an idyllic childhood that is available to many kids today. But few enjoy it. Today's kids spend a lot of time watching TV and playing computer games.

This is not the kid's fault, although it may be the parents fault, even though the culture has changed. So raising kids today has changed as well. The primary shift seems to be from activism to passivism. Kids sit and wait to be entertained. They expect the fun to come to them. We had to go out and find fun for ourselves. Although we had TV it was nothing like the TV of today. In our TV a man and women could not be shown in bed together even if they were married in real life. Recall in "I Love Lucy" they had twin beds and they were actually married in real life.

Today's TV is characterized by sex and violence, protected by the 1st Amendment. Parents, if they care, have to block these shows. They have to block websites as well. Thus, the onus is on the busy parents and not on some sort of community standards that determines what is on TV.

All this exposes kids to forces that did not exist in my day and makes parenting more difficult. Not only that, but both parents work today leaving little time for the quality time that kids need and want. Love is often expressed today by the parents buying their kids something they want like X-Boxes, Ipods, cell phones and the latest fashion jeans. We have had, since the end of WWII, the idea of keeping up with the Jones but now this idea has spread to the kids. Kids are now trying to keep up with each other by having the latest gadgets. Rather than working for them or by having good grades, they are given out of love by the parents.

All this produces kids with high expectations and who suffer little disappointment. When this disappointment comes to them in adult life, as it surely will, it will be a strange phenomenon. They will come to feel that they are being cheated out of some sort of birthright. Hostility towards society is often the result. In short their young lives, we do not prepare them for adulthood in many cases.

So now we have both parents working, returning home after a stressful drive in stop and go traffic, after having often worked for a bad boss in a stressful workplace and having to deal with kids who in many cases have gone wild. Not a parenting dream world.

Many kids desperately need attention. Often they misbehave to get this attention. My cats even misbehave to get attention when they are ignored. If cats can figure that out, surely children can.

In the 60's the motto of the boomers was "sex, drugs and rock and roll" and "tune in, turn on, and drop out". That seems to be the motto today. The one place that kids could get some discipline in their lives is at school. But the schools have softened under the Liberal agenda. Few kids are held back for failing to do the work and are promoted with the social promotion. Office workers claim to be too busy to deal with discipline problems and expect the teachers to take care of this. The teachers are working under the tenet that by being friends with the student, the student will behave so the teacher is reluctant to discipline the students for fear of breaking an established personal relationship with their students. School becomes a place where there is little discipline imposed. So if there is no discipline imposed at home, the kids have no discipline in their lives.

Schools have become daycare centers, a place for the kids to be while the parents work. But what about Saturday and Sunday when there is no school? Well the marketplace has come to the rescue with cartoons. Kids sit there frozen watching them. Then there are the commercials directed at kids, that completes the loop. The commercials show all the toys and gadgets that the parents can buy for them to show their love. Some include the message "get mom and dad to buy you one today." They stop short of saying the more effective message "if your mom and dad really loved you, they would buy you one of these."

So commercials during Saturday and Sunday and cartoon shows create the demand that is met by the parents to show their love in lieu of quality time. These commercials are not illegal and are, in fact, protected by the 1st amendment. Right thinking people might refuse to allow their kids watch the shows but then the kids would be underfoot. Easier is to just buy them the toy they want and be done with it.

I was once speaking with a Korean lady about this very subject. She told me that we have a simple philosophy about raising children – talk back, get spanking, obey teacher, do work. No amount of books of the subject could distill the essence of the matter any simpler than that.

Spanking was eliminated from child raising by Dr. Spock's famous book. In California there is legislation being put forth to make it a felony to spank your child. Spanking was removed from school as well. I was spanked and recommend it as a last resort. The other options are rejecting the child and telling them to leave your presence. The child then goes into their own room and plays with their TV or computer games and waits for you to cool off. They have experienced this before. Just wait. But this rejection itself is harmful. Better to spank them then hug them and tell them you love them.

The best way to discipline children is to take away their toys. Take away their cell phone. Now that's real punishment. Take away their Ipod and X-box. For example, I told you not to do that and you did it anyway. So no cell phone, X-box and Ipod for two weeks. Or try this. You made a D on your Math exam. So no cell phone, X-box and Ipod until you bring in a B on your next test.

One of my recommendations to the school board which they refused to even address was to require that all tests be brought home, singed by the parents and returned to the teacher the next day. This sounds so simple. The parents could follow their child's progress on nearly a daily basis. Then bad grades, no toys could be the rule. I am told that teachers, protected by the all powerful union would not want to deal with the hassle of doing this. Their contract is cleverly worded and says that any changes in "working conditions" must be approved by the teachers. Well, of course, any changes at all could be construed as changes in working conditions.

The point is that there are ways to punish your child and unless you are so liberal that you think children should not be punished for misbehaving, that punishment itself is harmful, it can be done. The problem with reasoning with kids is that they can't reason at early ages. Their minds have not developed to the point of understanding logic.

But we find discipline problems with kids who can reason, say, in high school. Reasoning does not seem to work. Removing cell phones, X-boxes and Ipods does work.

But is it being done? This should be part of the American culture. Every kid in the world should know that in America, if you misbehave, you lose your toys. We should be famous for that. Make no mistake about it, we have the power to control our kids. We just don't seem to want to do it. It seems that America is so rich, that we can afford the luxury of misbehaving kids.

The popular approach of grounding is often used. The child is sent to their room. But there they have their cell phone, X-box and Ipod plus their own TV in many cases. This is hardly punishment. Punishment would be to download a math test from the Internet and make them take it. Learning as punishment? No. Being made to do something that you do not like to do is punishment. Cut the grass. Wash the car. Vacuum the house, that's punishment. If harsh enough, the kids will quickly learn to behave.

So there are ways to discipline kids even in the face of all the external forces now in their lives. What it takes are disciplined parents. Disciplined parents produce disciplined kids. Therefore, when we see undisciplined kids, the parents are telegraphing to the world that they, themselves, have no discipline. This fits with their economic situation. They are often poor because they have no discipline and have had no discipline for their entire lives. Their children will imitate this behavior.

It can be shown scientifically that parenting is a learned behavior. They have taken newly born monkeys from the troop and raised them in a zoo or laboratory. When that monkey matures and has a baby, they do not know how to raise it. Why?

Because they have never seen it done. In the wild they will learn to imitate the behavior of female monkeys in their troop.

So one generation of bad parents in society is sufficient to produce many future generations of bad parents. The WWII generation produced the boomers. They are now the grandparents of today's misbehaving children while the boomers' children are their parents. Perhaps parents today do not know how to be good parents because they have never seen it done. They are simply doing to their kids, what their parents did to them. At the advice of Dr. Spock they were never spanked so they do not spank their kids. Their parents did not take away their toys for misbehaving so they do not take away their children's toys for misbehaving.

Combine this with the "everybody is doing it" rationale and it becomes a lost cause. Many parents just suffer through it until the kid graduates and moves out. In many cases when the kid fails at life, for lack of a proper upbringing, they move back in. That possibility alone is enough to make you want to discipline your kids.

Another dimension to this might be the lack of grandparents. He grandparent/child link is very important and basic to the family structure. This has been changed by nursing homes. The grandparents, where the wisdom is, are often apart from their grandchildren on a daily basis, being confined to nursing homes. When growing up I was more ashamed to have my grandparents find out about my poor performance in school than I was to have my parents find out. Getting lectured by my grandparents had a dimension that was missing when getting lectured by my parents. "Let's go talk to grandma and grandpa about this" sent chills up my spine.

Finally, we have the fat child epidemic. Many children are seriously overweight. This is partly due to the fact that they sit around watching TV or playing with their computer games rather than getting exercise and partly due to their diet. Big Macs and pizzas, although enjoyable to eat, are fattening foods. Even the meals that they eat in school are not that healthy as I have already commented on. A lot of this is due to the fact that the parents are overweight as well. We are a fat nation. If the parents are overweight, they have little motivation to see that their kids are not. The parents eat the Big Macs and pizzas too. You can't very well tell you kids to eat their vegetables while you are eating a pizza.

The problem is, like so many problems today, that both parents work. This is because the American Empire has lost all its wealth because of bad decisions by unwise politicians so now both parents have to work to survive. It becomes very easy to just stop by on the way home and pick up a few happy meals or a pizza, otherwise, you have to go home, tired after a long day's work, and cook supper.

There are several problems to being overweight as a child. First, is the physical health problem. Many of today's kids are expected to be diabetic at age 40. It has been predicted that diabetes will be a national epidemic in 30 years. This will be Type II diabetes and directly related to body weight. In type II diabetes, your body can get so big, that your pancreas cannot make enough insulin to supply your body with what it needs. This is why diabetics are told to lose weight.

Harmful also is the children's mental health. When they reach puberty they will begin being attracted to the opposite sex. Our society places a great deal of emphasis on having a good figure. Fat girls and fat boys are not physically attractive in today's world. Therefore, these kids will suffer sexual rejection at puberty. This has long lasting effects.

Although I am a conservative, I think that America should use the schools as an opportunity to give the kids who want it a free breakfast and free lunch at school. At least we could guarantee them two healthy meals a day, assuming that we could improve school menus. The increase in government spending for this would be offset by the reduced food bills of the parents. Then there is also the savings to society if we can avoid the diabetes epidemic that is being predicted.

Chapter 21

Religion in America

"Everyday people are straying from the church and going back to God." - Lenny Bruce

American has a long history as a religious country. The Declaration of Independence speaks of "nature's God" and of rights endowed by our "creator". The President and most office holders take their oath on a bible. There are morning prayers in both the Senate and the House. All branches of the military have chaplains and there are churches on most military bases. Our money has printed on it "In God we trust".

Yet of late, much of America seems to have rejected religion. There are movements, successful movements, to remove religion from schools. Many reject the Boy Scouts as an organization that embraces religion. The end of the Boy Scout oath is "brave, clean and reverent."

The most famous statement used by those who want to rid America of religion is taken from a letter written by Thomas Jefferson. In the letter he said "we have built a wall separating church and state." Thus, from that letter, the expression "separation of church and state" derives. It should be noted that this was a private letter written by Thomas Jefferson to a group of religious people and this phrase appears in no official government documents. It was Jefferson who recognized "natures' God" and a "creator" in the Declaration of independence.

What the Founding Fathers intended was that there was to be no official government religion and that people were free to practice any religion they wished or to practice no religion at all if that was their wish. These people were Liberals in the traditional sense and not in the modern day sense. They believed in freedom. (Curiously, today's Liberals believe in big government which of necessity, limits personal freedom given all the laws, rules and regulations that must be adhered to.)

Yet with no official state religion, the vast majority of people believed that there was a God who could be worshipped in any way that free people wanted to worship.

Today a few atheists, about 2% to 5% of the population, using the activist judges in the leftist dominated courts, to try to stamp out religion all together. This is being done in government related organizations like schools and other public, albeit government, sponsored functions.

A federal judge recently ruled that the national day of prayer was unconstitutional.

They readily admit that we are free to practice religion in private in the way that the early Christians had to do in secret before the Roman Empire converted to Christianity.

Even retail merchandisers recently issued orders to their employees not to say "Merry Christmas" but merely "Happy Holidays" to their customers. This shows that they thought that there are many people who spend money that support the anti-God movement in today's America. But they were wrong. Under public outrage they rescinded that policy.

A lot of this is due to religious people themselves. We have witnessed sex scandals in the Catholic Church. Before that there was Tammy Baker and her husband and the scandals that they were involved in by spending their church's money on luxuries. Several radio ministers were involved in sex scandals. All of this has made certain religious people look like hypocrites. Add to this that religion calls for restraint and moral behavior. Everything that we might call fun today is often forbidden by religion. I am referring to free sex (promiscuity), pornography, mind altering, or mood altering, drugs and sexy dress to name a few. Since religion rejects these things, many people reject religion. It is all about fun these days after all. After all, it's a party living in America.

The Founding Fathers understood that the people would always get what they wanted. What was hard to predict was that what people would be made to want by TV commercials and a culture gone mad and protected by the 1st amendment. These things appealed to prurient interests. (def - arousing or appealing to unusual or unwholesome sexual desires) This is what Abraham Lincoln would have called the darker angels of our nature. But we live in a capitalist economy and these things sell. Indeed, they create jobs.

So religion is on decline as the good times go on. This, despite the fact that churches do many good things. They care for the homeless, they support groups like the Boy Scouts and Girl Scouts, and they provide recreational services for the elderly and provide food for the hungry.

The nice thing about God is that he is there for you if you want him. But many people do not want him. People do turn to God when they are suffering. For example, people with a serious illness often turn to God. Often their illness comes from not holding to the tenets of religion in the first place. For example, alcoholics, heroin addicts, most AIDS victims have brought on these illnesses themselves by abusing their bodies. Now they expect the God, who they have ignored all their lives, to step in and heal them with a miracle. Miracles happen often enough to make this seem feasible.

The dimension of religion in a culture adds long standing truths to people's thinking. If there were nothing but the

Golden Rule and the Ten Commandments to follow people's lives would be improved. One could even forget the teachings of Jesus, Buddha and Mohammed and just follow the Golden Rule. Is it asking too much that you treat people in the way that you would like to be treated? Well apparently so.

Most religious teachings are common sense and easily supported by logic. But churches often go beyond this common sense. Many people think that religions want control over them. Many resent this.

So what would cause a turnaround in religious decline? The good news is that this is possible. The bad news is that suffering causes this change. As people suffer they turn to God for relief. As long as this suffering can be held off, the turn to God does not take place. America's leadership realizes this .They also realize the suffering by the voters will put them out of office. Curiously what is good for religious growth is bad for political stability. There is, thus, a real separation of church and state. What we need is a sudden great disaster but things happen slowly and people get used to the change.

But there may be hope. I was teaching an 11th grade class one day. They were studying knights and the Middle Ages. They were each to make a shield containing things they believed in. Something like a family crest or coat of arms. That day they were to present their shields to the class. One by one they went to the front of the room to explain their shields. "I have a book here because I like to read." "I have a tree here because I like nature and the woods." To my surprise several said "I have a cross here because I believe in God." This began to happen so often that I asked a student if the teacher had told them to address this. The student said that no, the teacher did not mention it. So I ask her why so many kids have a cross on their shield and say that they believe in God. She said "Because they believe in God." Duh was implied. Remember these were 11th graders. A warm feeling came over me.

So apparently this is something that kids talk about even if or perhaps especially since it is banned from schools.

So religion is not dead, it has simply been removed from public places like schools. People can still worship if they want but religion is under attack. There are major battles left to fight by the Left in this regard. Here are a few:

- There could be a movement to take "In God We Trust" off of our money.

- There could be a movement to stop spending taxpayer's dollars paying the salaries of chaplains in the military. This is state supported religion.

- There could be a movement to remove churches from military bases. This is again state supported religion.

- There could be a movement to end the property tax exemption that churches now enjoy. This, too, is state supported religion making other people's taxes higher.

- There could be a movement to make contributions to churches no longer deductible from our income taxes. Once again state supported religion.

- There could be a movement to remove "under God" from the Pledge of Allegiance.

This was actually tried in the liberal 9th circuit court of appeals. They ruled that children could not say the pledge because it says "under God". They agued that this was a fairly recent addition. I remember being in grade school when one day the teacher told us that we were going to start saying the pledge in a new way. This would have been around 1953. This ruling was overturned on appeal in the midst of much public outrage.

None of these things subsidize any particular religion rather religion in general. But the anti-religious movement is more an anti-God movement since it's the atheists that are behind it. The force to eliminate religion from public places is not anti-Catholic, or anti-Christian, or anti-Jewish or anti-Muslim but it's anti-God.

The idea of God goes back a long way in human history. People have always had Gods. Even those primitive tribes often discovered in remote jungles are found to have a God. This is because there are some things that are simply not understandable through science and can only be attributed to God. It makes sense but makes God not understandable either. What is God? Nobody knows. People debate the issue but do not resolve it. Whatever it is, it is the cause of things that we don't understand. As we understand these things, that aspect of God goes away. For example, we no longer have a rain God because we know what causes rain.

We in the world now only have one God who has many aspects rather than many Gods who specialize. There was once a God of Love. Love is still something that we don't understand but the God of Love went away and the God, a super God, is responsible for love. Some say God is Love.

Science cannot explain where the universe came from. For religious people the answer is simple – God created it. Though we know where babies come from, to many people God has given us a baby.

The chief problem with God is explaining all the terrible things that happen. Why would God let hurricanes kill people, including innocent little children? It is explained that God works in mysterious ways, his wonders to perform. It is assumed that we are not meant to understand this process. Only God knows. We, on the other hand, must have faith. That's our job.

So we are faced with a totally not understandable God who is responsible for many things, good and bad, and this idea of God goes back to the beginning of mankind. Could the approximately nine billion people who have ever lived have been wrong? One thing that we can say about God is that he is not going away.

There are currently efforts to put religion back into schools as Philosophy. Here we would tell the students that many people think that there is a God. Then we discuss the history of God, like the Greek and Roman Gods. Then we discuss prophets, people who claimed to have spoken to God. Moses, Jesus and Mohammed are examples. Then we discuss the differences in the various religions and the varying beliefs. Then we discuss the great philosophers and what they though about this. This approach does not endorse a particular religion nor does it endorse religion in general. It would be a combination philosophy and history course. But it would introduce kids to religion then we tell the students that you can take it or leave it. It would be an elective course so that the children of atheists would not even have to take the course.

This is a common sense solution but offered at a time where there is little common sense. Recall that I stated earlier that there are people who do not want to see a given problem go away since they derive their income dealing with the problem. This may happen here as those who are interested in removing God from society are not interested in a compromise that makes the problem go away. Perhaps there is profit in Atheism. Perhaps Atheism creates jobs.

The question is how can such a small amount of people, the atheists, have enough power to tell the vast majority of people how to worship? Admitted atheists are about 2% to 5% of the population. Well the pendulum is swinging back from the liberalism of the 60's to conservatism. Right now it is passing through the center. This means that America is split about 50/50 or more like 51/49. Elections are very close as the 2000 Florida presidential election proved. At 51/49 this means that 2% of the voters can swing the election either way. Thus no one running for office can afford to alienate even 2% of the population.

Thus the atheists, like gays have power beyond their numbers. And they are using their power, buttressed by the courts and their activist judges, to remove God from the public space. Notice that this is more than anti-religious. The issue of nativity scenes on city hall could have been resolved by allowing all religious groups to display their artifacts. Make it a universal celebration of religion. But that would have still been God in the public space.

The increasing in diversity in our society plays its role here too. The recent immigrants come from places like the Middle East and Asia whose religions are vastly different from ours. Should Muslim school children be allowed to pray 4 times a day while in school?

Chapter 22

The Great Religious War

"We had better dispense with the personification of evil, because it leads, all too easily, to the most dangerous kind of war: religious war."
Konrad Lorenz

The next great danger, apart from America destroying herself from within through bad decisions, is the Great Religious War. This is the war between radical Islam and the West with America being the foremost symbol of the West.

I will discuss their culture so the reader will see how we differ from our enemy.

The issues are very complicated given the vast differences between Middle Eastern and Western cultures. We simply do not understand each other. I was in the Middle East for 4 months. This was my first exposure to that part of the world and the first thing I noticed was the unbearable heat. The men all wear white and the women all wear black. The women's heads are covered with only a small slit for them to see through. It is very strange walking down the street. We called the women BMOs (black moving objects).

So the first difference I noticed was the total lack of fashion although there are very cheap and very expensive versions of what they wear, but westerners can't tell the difference. Fashion is very important part of Western culture with very few people wearing the same outfit two days in a row. Where their women wear sandals, our women have dozens of pairs of high heeled shoes. While on the subject of shoes, the greatest insult you can pay an Arab is to show them the sole of your shoe. I was warned repeatedly about this. We men have a way of sitting with one leg laying horizontally across the other. This stance of necessity exposes the bottom of the shoe. I caught myself doing that many times. A strange way to insult people and it's the equivalent of giving someone the finger in the West.

I enjoyed the food which was very tasty and healthy. I was doing business there and learned a lot about how they do business. First, nothing is ever settled. The deal is completed only after money has actually changed hands and it's too late to get the money back. Any verbal arrangement and even contracts are up for renegotiation and change until the money actually changes hands. This explains the problem that we had negotiating with Yassar Arifat who was always backing out of deals that were made verbally. To him this is how business is done. What was said yesterday has little to do with today especially if something changed last night.

We, on the other hand depend on agreements and contracts to lock things in and the changing hands of money is a formality once the deal is made. This is our business culture, theirs is totally different.

An interesting idea they have is Islamic banking. The Koran forbids charging interest as we do in the West. So how do banks make loans? The bank lends you money and becomes a partner in your business. They will share in the profits and this, with the payback of the principal, makes the bank a profit. This means that it is in the bank's interest that you succeed in your business and they will help you do that. They use their contacts to help you succeed so they will not only get the principal back, but some of your profits as "interest."

In the West a bank might make a loan to you and also make a loan to your competitor also. Giving your competitor a loan is actually against your business interests but the Western banks make money off of both of you.

I went to open a bank account. Saving accounts are easy but a checking account is more difficult. You have to be recommended by another customer of the bank. If you bounce a check and refuse to make it good, the bank will go to the person who recommended you and request that they make it good. If that person refuses the bank will go to the person who recommended him and ask them to make it good. All along this gets embarrassing for everyone who are seen as recommending a deadbeat. It usually gets taken care of at the lowest level. So there are few bounced checks.

Crime was virtually unheard of. Punishment is very, very strict. They could lock you away for a very long time, cut off your hand or cut off your head. You are perfectly safe walking the streets at any time of the day or night and in any neighborhood. When there is an issue to deal with the police appear and says the equivalent of "freeze". Anyone who runs is shot, the thinking being that if he wasn't guilty, then why did he run? In America that would guarantee that the policeman would brought up on charges. There the policeman might get an award for a job well done.

If your dog bites someone who is not on your property, the police come and shoot your dog. That is the end of it. So people keep their dogs well locked up.

In Bahrain I saw some beautiful mansions generally made of marble. People had marble driveways. The sides of their mansion were marble as were the floors inside. The Holiday Inn I stayed at was solid marble. But next to a beautiful mansion might be a junk yard or a mini-mall. They have no sense of zoning. There was a large, oil pipeline that ran through the front yards of a long line of beautiful mansions. Residents had to drive across a little bridge to get to their house. Nobody seemed to mind. Their attitude is that this is my home and I can't be held responsible for what is around me. I have no control over that.

So you can see how we differ and to try to understand them in terms of our own beliefs is impossible. Yet we are forced by circumstance to deal with these people and now those relationships have taken a sharp turn toward a very threatening place.

First, if we did not get our much needed oil from there, we would ignore them completely and they would live in 800AD.

The West has always meddled in the Middle East beginning when that area was a part of the trade routes to the East –India and China. The British Empire dominated the place and built the Suez canal. They built railroads as well. Lawrence of Arabia, a British officer wanted to unite all of Arabia into one country and thought that he had the blessing of his government to do that, but the British decided that having them as a bunch of feuding tribes would make it easier to control hem. If you look at a map of the Middle East you will see a lot of straight lines, rather than so called natural boundaries caused by rivers and mountain ranges. This is because those boundaries were drawn in the British Foreign Office with a ruler. The British actually created those countries and their boundaries.

When WWII ended, the Jews, given the suffering that they endured as the West initially looked the other way, felt that they were due their own homeland. They wanted it to be their historical homeland which was Palestine. The British obliged and eventually Israel was formed.

To understand the significance of that in Arab terms you have to remember two things. First, the Arab people can trace their heritage continuously back to the Roman Empire. In Europe their Roman heritage was interrupted by the Dark Ages which lasted until the Renaissance. Although this is continuous history, it is not a continuous heritage in the cultural sense. By comparison, Americans can only trace their culture back a couple of hundred years.

So the Arabs see their history as one long continuous unpunctuated event. The second thing to remember is that Arabia, in addition to a long history of being dominated by Europe, was invaded many times by the Crusaders. European armies actually invaded and killed many of their people. They then see Israel as a permanent European settlement in their land and are determined to remove this permanent settlement. Accordingly, they see America's wars like the Kuwaiti war and now the Iraqi and Afghanistan wars as just another invasion from the West and exactly like another crusade, only this time led by the Americans rather than the Europeans. We, of course, don't see it that way. Thus, there is a great misunderstanding between us.

Accordingly, they see our support for Israel, who drove the Palestinians off their lands, as our support for a Western settlement in their land. The Israelis see their occupancy of Palestine as land that was won fairly in war and in a war that they did not start. Throughout history land was won in war and was kept by the victors as the fruits of the victory. Nearly every country in the world was formed that way including America, who took the land from the Indians.

These views continued with a minor war from time to time for a long time. But now a fundamental change has taken place. Radical Muslims have sensed that the West is weak and in decline. And they are right. They think that now is the time to strike. They have the manpower and are close to the oil fields that we need. If they can get control of the oil they can, bring the West to its knees. To do that, they will have to topple Middle-East governments that are friendly to the West. To do that they will need gorilla armies. This was the model that caused America to lose the Viet Nam war.

They have the people and all they need is a cause to unite them. Israel is the cause. This will, they know, have to be an unconventional war because they do not have cruise missiles and supersonic jet fighters and bombers. American once fought an unconventional war against the British to win her independence. The radical Muslims see this as exactly the same thing.

As for the use of suicide bombers, the Japanese used these in WWII. As for the killing of civilians, the Americans and British bombed German cities ruthlessly during WWII killing many civilians. The cruelest was the fire bombing of Dresden. Thousands of civilians were burned to death including children and old people. So the West has killed its share of innocent civilians.

As far as the development of nuclear weapons goes there is this argument. Israel has nuclear weapons so why can't we? Suppose this compromise is put forward. Let's make the Middle East a nuclear free zone. We will stop our development of nuclear weapons and Israel will give up her nuclear weapons and agree to inspections to verify compliance. Sounds fair except that Israel will never give up her nuclear weapons. They are their ace in the hole that Israel will never be destroyed. So that compromise is out.

How about if we setup a homeland for the Palestinians? Many attempts have been made to do that. Jordan even turned over the entire West bank to them. Israel claims to want this but that may only be lip services. If there was a Palestinian homeland then it would be sovereign country. This means that it could have an army. The homeland would get much support from the rich Arab states so it would have a fine army. Probably not as good as Israel's armed forces since they enjoy having the finest American weapons. We would not make those weapons available to the Palestinians. They would have to get their weapons from the French and the Russians.

What if there was a war? Given that Israel has nuclear weapons Israel would ultimately win that war. So what if Palestine got nuclear weapons from, say, Iran? Well now we would be back to the MAD theory. MAD stands for Mutually Assured Destruction. This is what prevented nuclear war during the cold war. Both sides knew that they would be destroyed in such a war. MAD worked.

This would be the case if the Palestinians had nuclear weapons. Neither side would be able to use them. In this case, either side would pollute their own lands with radio activity. That pollution would made the land uninhabitable a century. Thus, neither side could or would use them. If there was a war it would be a conventional war as all the wars in that part of the world have been. Israel, with the better weapons would win that war. Plus the Palestinians would be busy for years just establishing their new country. They would not have time to think about war for a long time. So why don't they have a homeland? This would take a lot of the pressure off that part of the world.

So our arguments to them seem hypocritical as if the radical Muslims are being held to a different standard than soldiers in previous wars. It seems unfair. Talking, as so many recommend, may be fruitless. First, our general outlooks are vastly different owing to our cultural differences.

Removing Israel is out of the question. Anything we recommend is going to look one-sided and not a fair deal. War seems the only solution but we are not winning the war. Our hands are tied by our own softness and by a division in the American public. Like all wars, the most vicious generally win and we are not the most vicious. Not only that, we do not even have a cause to rally our people behind. They have a cause and it is getting Western influence out of their lands. The people will rally behind this cause. What do we have? The survival of Israel? How many Westerners really care about that and are willing to die for it? We do have the economic cause of continuing to get the oil but nobody wants to say that all this killing is over oil. We need a moral cause. 9/11 gave us that and stopping the terrorist became the Clarion call. 9/11 was a big tactical error on their part and Bin Laden took the heat for it. Their cause is so strong that their people are willing to commit suicide for it while we have trouble raising funding for the war.

This is why we have not had any more terrorist attacks here. The word has been put out. The American public is turning against the war. We want that trend to continue. So no terrorist attacks that would unite the American people and change their thinking. When the Americans pull out of Iraq and Afghanistan as they will surely do, then we can start the terrorist attacks as payback. We have to win this war, they only have to keep it going until we grow tired.

This makes the speech from President Bush curiously correct. We are fighting them over there so that we do not have to fight them over here. And they will follow us home if we pull out.

This is one of those great turning points in history. We can't leave Iraq and Afghanistan without having terrorist attacks here and we can't stay in Iraq and Afghanistan either. This was an ill-conceived operation from the beginning as was the Viet Nam war. (But it does create jobs.) There they had the strong moral cause of uniting their country, we had the weaker cause of stopping communist aggression.

When the body bags start coming home only a strong moral cause will do.

Chapter 23

America's Energy Policy and Global Warming

"There is not the slightest indication that energy will ever be obtainable from the atom"
- Albert Einstein

Much is being said about America's energy policy or perhaps America's lack of energy of an energy policy. Every time the price of gas goes up, the people blame the government as if the government, and not the marketplace, sets the price of gasoline. Yet if the government demanded that people drive smaller cars, then the cry would be that our freedom to drive whatever we want is being taken away. Americans have been spoiled by everyone, including our leaders, by telling us how great we are. We want it all and we want it now.

The government's position on this is that you are free to buy a big car and spend any or all of your money on gas if you want to. People who choose big SUVs might pay over $100 for a fill up but it their money and they can spend it as they like. This is true.

But the government does have a role to play in the price of gas. For example, the government can assure that there is no gouging going on and that there is no collusion on the part of the big oil companies to set the price of gas.

In the 50's there were gas wars with filling stations making their gas a penny or two cheaper than the station across the street. This forced that station to lower their prices. When you filled up, not only did they check your oil and clean your windshield but they gave you a set of drinking glasses or a piece of tableware. If you shopped at the same station you could collect the whole set, dishes, cups & saucers, salad bowl, etc.

Now we pump our own gas and check our own oil. Done cleverly, there is a often a self serve pump and a full serve pump. And it's your choice. Curiously this means that the rich get all these services and the poor do not. Things always seem to work out that way.

So what happened to those days? I suspect that there was real competition in those days and I suspect that there is not real competition today.

Over my lifetime I have heard many excuses for gas price hikes. Once there was a shortage of oil so the price of gas naturally goes up. Once there was an abundance of oil and gas prices went up. Why? Well it seems that with an abundance of oil, storage costs went up and that increased cost must be passed on to the consumer as higher gas prices. This means that when there is a shortage of oil, gas prices go up and when there is an abundance of oil gas prices go up too. How do we win?

This last excuse is a nice touch – there is a shortage of refinery capacity because the oil companies are doing maintenance on refineries. It's curious that they chose the summer driving season to start doing maintenance on their refineries.

Often the excuse in the winter is that they are making home heating oil for the cold winter being expected thus the price of gas will go up due to a shortage of oil remaining after home heating oil is produced. The frustrating thing is that they always have an excuse. Sometimes it's because there is unrest in the Middle East. Sometimes it's OPEC's fault. Sometimes there is a shortage of tankers to haul the oil. The fact is that a big component of the price of gas is federal, state and local taxes.

The fact is that we do not have an energy policy and that is the government's fault. States like Florida refuse to allow off shore drilling where we know there is American oil. Massachusetts is fighting the use of windmills off Cape Cod and the Kennedy's are agreeing since it might spoil the view from their compound at Hyannis Port.

Environmentalists are fighting another Alaska pipeline which would bring us more Alaska oil. Or would it? Much of Alaska's oil goes to Japan because the transportation costs to ship it there are less than to ship it to the refineries in Los Angeles. For every barrel of Alaska oil (American oil) shipped to Japan we import another barrel of foreign oil to make up the difference. We see the whole world as one giant barrel of oil.

We have not built an oil refinery in this country in nearly 30 years despite the increase in demand for gas during that time. It seems that nobody wants a dirty refinery around them. So why don't we build the refineries on the government land in Nevada? Nobody lives there and it's close to the West coast markets.

Detroit is way behind in making hybrid cars while the Japanese have several on the market already. Then there are the ethanol fuels made from corn. Brazil runs all its cars using this technology. Where are we? Well the increased demand for corn for gasoline drives up the price of corn and everything that is produced from corn, like Corn Flakes and even liquor.

What happened to solar energy? Although you can't run your car on it, it can be used to preheat hot water for homes reducing energy costs.

Much electricity is made by burning oil. This oil could be made into gasoline for cars. In WWII, the Germans made synthetic oil from coal. We have a lot of coal.

People will say that it's the economics. Oil is cheaper than other forms of energy. There are some fallacies in that argument. First, the economic model being used does not factor in the cost of our risk from depending on foreign oil. This is because that dollar amount is hard to compute. For example, how much risk are we incurring by importing 60% of our oil. Without it the economy would collapse and the cost to society would be great. So only if the risk is slight, the number is large when you multiply that small risk by the number that represents to cost of a great depression. And there is a risk since much of our imported oil comes from unstable parts of the world. Factor in that number and solar could be cheaper than oil.

Secondly, the government determines what is cheaper by its taxing policy. For a long time the oil companies enjoyed the Oil Depletion Allowance which gave them a tax break and made oil cheaper than other forms of energy. So by its taxing policy, the government determines what forms of energy are the least expensive. Thanks to the Oil Depletion Allowance, the oil companies built their infrastructure. Any competing form of energy would have to build their own infrastructure and pass those capital costs to the consumer. This would make their form of energy more expensive than oil so our dependency on oil continues.

This argument is often put forward. Many retirement plans and mutual funds have their assets in oil company stocks. If those stock prices fell due to genuine competition with other forms of energy, then those pension funds would be in trouble.

There is a great truth about energy. It is that a barrel saved is exactly equal to a barrel pumped. So rather than importing, say, 50 million barrels why don't we save 50 million barrels? This could be accomplished by driving smaller cars. But now we hit the wall – the American culture.

Americans are power oriented people. Actually, they have little power as individuals but are made to think they have. This is how the average citizen shares in America's power. You could argue that since America is the most powerful country in the world then American citizens are the most powerful citizens in the world. Americans like power. We see power being offered in movies with these great explosions. In our last war Americans could watch buildings being destroyed by smart bombs which have a TV camera in their nose. It's fun to watch power in action.

So naturally Americans want power in the daily lives. The way to get this is to drive a powerful car. Car commercials exploit this. What we see are fast cars in the commercials. These cars hug the road at high speeds and accelerate from zero to sixty in seconds. The off road vehicles are powerful too. Like tanks they can go anywhere. Power is great. That's what I want, a big powerful off road vehicle that can go anywhere. Nothing can stop me because I am powerful. The fact that it costs me $100 per fill up is the government's fault. We'll take care of that in the next election.

It is very difficult to change culture. People are literally programmed by the TV commercials they watch. We are not the only country where citizens feel that they are powerful. The average Roman citizen felt powerful and did the average German citizen in WWII. Giving the citizenry, a sense of individual power is a good way for the government to stay in power. Making citizens feel powerless plants the seeds of revolution. The American Revolution was due in part that the colonists felt powerless against British domination. Taxation without representation is tyranny.

Power is a big component of an American's psyche and their car is the way they project this power. So getting Americans into small cars will be a problem. The marketplace is supposed to take care of things like this. As the price of gas goes up people will start driving smaller cars. So what happened to the marketplace?

What happened is that the price of energy is a part of the cost of living. The cost of living is a consideration in determining increases in many pensions and is a factor in labor contract negotiations. So many people effectively get a raise when gas prices go up. This cancels the effect of the price increase leaving little motivation to conserve fuel by driving a small car. As labor costs go up via union contracts, it tends to push everyone's salaries up. If labor gets a raise, then management gets a raise also. A rising tide does lift all boats.

The solution would be not to consider energy costs in cost of living issues and that is what the government did. They found and excuse not to include energy (and food) in the cost of living index. If food prices soar the government does not think we need a raise. The same is true for energy. So as the price of gas goes up, then salaries won't keep up. This would force people to cut back on energy consumption. Would the oil companies like that? Of course not. They sell oil and like anyone in business, they want to sell as much of their product as possible. The Oil companies are not interested in people using less oil and would be against any legislation that would eventually result in that.

Also, if they sell less oil, they will have to charge more for it because they have fixed costs and they must make enough money to pay their fixed costs. So if we all drove small cars, the price of gas would actually go up. (Electricity costs will increase if we use less electricity; water costs will increase if we use less water; natural gas costs will increase if we use less natural gas. Fixed expenses by these companies have to be recovered and on fewer unit sales of their product. Thus they have to charge more per unit.)

Suppose the government wants to make solar energy as cheap as oil through some legislation. The oil companies would be against that legislation. This is not particularly wrong. Lobbying and campaign contributions are, in fact, legal. Protecting your interests is human nature.

What is takes to counteract these powerful interests is an angry voter.

Recent gas price rises resulting in government's considering reducing the tax component in the price of a gallon of gas. This policy would abate public anger but actually encourage gas consumption. This is certainly a policy that the oil companies would support. The government also considered tapping into our oil reserves being saved for the military in time of war. This policy too would have made more oil available and kept its price down. But this oil is for true emergencies.

These government actions are exactly opposite to what they should be doing. They should be implementing policies to reduce oil consumption, not keep it the same.

The military-industrial complex benefits too from our dependence on foreign oil. As long as we have that dependence, we will need a strong military to guarantee future oil supplies.

Now let's look at global warming. What is causing that? I will offer this scientific explanation.

If you spin a top on the floor you will notice that it warbles, that is, it does not stay perfectly vertical when it spins. This motion is called "precession" by the physicists. The Earth also warbles on its North/South axis because of the gravitational pull of the Moon and the Sun. Thus, the line through the North and South poles inscribes a circle in the heavens. How long does it take this line to run 360 degrees around this inscribed circle (the period of precession)? About 26,000 years (exactly 25,770 years). This causes several phenomena. First, the North Star, Polaris, has not and will not always be the star that the Earth's axis points to. In 13,000 years it will be Vegas. Second, during this 26,000 years, the Earth's axis runs through the stars of 12 constellations in the sky (the Zodiac) and this is the basis of astrology. We are coming into the Age of Aquarius, 2013, from the Age of Pisces due to this precession. Each age lasts 2000+ years. The birth of Christ coincides approximately with the start of the Age of Pisces. Many people think that great things happen at the start of each new age. Thus the song lyric "This is the dawning of the Age of Aquarius".

This change in the tilt of the Earth causes the Northern hemisphere to face closer to or farther from the Sun over this 26,000 year period. This, along with a couple of other things (see next paragraph), causes the ice ages and global warming (melting ice caps) in the Northern hemisphere.

But there is more. The Earth's orbit around the Sun varies from nearly circular to very elliptical over a period of 21,000 years. When very elliptical the winters are very cold since the Earth gets very far from the Sun and the summers are very hot since the Earth gets very close to the Sun. Then there is the 41,000 year cycle of *obliquity,* the tilt of the Earth's axis with respect to a direction perpendicular to its orbital plane. From time to time all these things come together to put the Northern hemisphere as far from the Sun as it can possibly get and there is an ice age. (search Google for Milankovitch Cycles to learn more.) Also, these things sometimes come together to place the Northern hemisphere as close to the Sun as it will ever get and this causes global warming in the Northern hemisphere. That is what melts ice from the ice age.

What this theory explains is what caused the last ice age, about 20,000 years ago, to end. Then there were no cars, no factories, and thus no man-made pollution. So what caused it to come to an end? Also, what causes ice ages to be periodic - one around every 20,000 years?

So it is not a simple as stop driving SUVs although man-made pollution may contribute to the problem but it can't be the major cause of global warming in the face of these other forces.

See a visual on precession at
http://csep10.phys.utk.edu/astr161/lect/time/precession.html
See the ice age graph caused by precession at http://www.museum.state.il.us/exhibits/ice_ages/precession_graph.html
Read about Milankovitch Cycles at
http://aa.usno.navy.mil/faq/docs/seasons_orbit.html

The Greeks first observed precession. Imagine with no telescopes. These were bright people.

Today, we know exactly where we are during this 26,000 precession cycle and the other Milankovitch Cycles. This is all backed up with Math and many renown scientists agree with this.

The Serbian astrophysicist Milutin Milankovitch (1879-1958) figured all this out. He is, as Sir Isaac Newton put it, one of the giants on whose shoulders we stand.

We all know our astrological sign but not where it comes from – precession.

So Al Gore's theory should be looked at with a jaundice eye, especially in light of the news that scientists had massaged their data in that is being called "climategate".

Chapter 24

The Stock Market

"If stock market experts were so expert, they would be buying stock, not selling advice." - Norman R. Augustine

How does one measure a society's successful functioning? How do we say that one society is better than another society? What do we look at? During the Hoover administration, the catch-phrase was "the business of America is business." But of course Hoover was the President when the great depression began. But that thinking seems to continue to this date. We are about making money. The people who founded this country came here to make money. Immigrants come to make money. Making money is often called "having a better life" and that interpretation implies that money is the secret to a good life. Philosophers would disagree. They talk about happiness, self-fulfillment and peace of mind as the things that result in a better life.

Suppose we came up with an index to evaluate societies and we calculated that index for all societies. Where would America fall in that list? Well that depends on how the index is structured. If per capita income was given a high weight in the index, then America would be at the top of the list. But if you include things like high school dropout rate, per capita illegal drug use, scores on standardized math tests, number of illegitimate births and teenage suicide then where would America fall on that list? If those things had a negative impact in the index, as they should, then America would certainly not be at the top. We are around 25th in math scores when compared with the rest of the world. Several of the things above put at the 3rd world level.

So is it all about money? You might think so if you look at the index we used to measure our success. This is the Dow Jones Industrial Average and seems to be what we look at. If the DOW is high, things are good, despite our high school dropout rate and illegal drug use. The focus of everyone in power is the DOW. This is the right thing to do if you think that the business of America is business. This keeps everyone employed but does this keep everyone happy?

Illegal drug use and legal alcohol use are often and indicators of the number of people who want to escape from reality. The logical conclusion would be "why aren't they happy with their reality"? What is so bad about one's reality that they feel the need to escape from it? A lot, perhaps most, of these people have jobs. Thus, they have money. Why isn't their money buying them happiness? Why do they need drugs to escape? The inescapable conclusion is that money does not buy happiness. If it did then there would be no suicides among rich people. Yet many rich people commit suicide.

If money does not buy happiness then should our thinking be that the business of America is business? Perhaps the business of America should be setting up a society where people can raise their families and be happy. In the early days of America, say up to the industrial revolution, this is the way it was. People lived on farms, raised their families and were happy. There was no DOW by which to measure our success.

The industrial revolution was perhaps the greatest change ever made in the America. People left the farms for a job in the city. People began working in factories and on assembly lines rather than working the fields. Cities became overpopulated as housing could not keep up. It is no accident that when looking at the blue states at the county level, we see that it is actually the big cities that are blue. The Democrats with their social programs have their power in the big cities. This is understandable since the poverty is in the big cities. The crime is in the big cities. Illegal drug use is in the big cities. I can go on an on. This is not to say that none of this happens in small towns because it does but not to the degree that it occurs in the big cities.

Are people in the big cities happy? Perhaps, since there are many things to buy, assuming that happiness can be purchased. Yet nearly all the psychiatrists are in the big cities. There are far more psychiatrists per thousand people in the big cities than in small town America. Since psychiatrists help troubled people, we can conclude that there are more unhappy people in the big cities. If the number of psychiatrists per thousand people was the same all over America, we could not come to that conclusion.

Apparently the thinking that the business of America is business has produced a lot of unhappy people and should be reexamined. Perhaps a rising DOW is not a valid measure of the goodness of a society. Other indices have been created but one rarely hears about them outside of academia. What we need is to have a Presidential candidate to endorse one of these indices and make it a part of his or her campaign. Then we could compare ourselves, not only to other societies, but to other times in our own history. Then we could see if things are getting better or if things are getting worse.

This was actually done by the Democrats when they come up with the famous "misery index". It was calculated by adding the inflation rate to the unemployment rate. The idea was that both inflation and unemployment hurt not only the poor but the nation in general This was used to show what a bad job the Republicans were doing. Then that index turned against the Democrats and showed that that the misery index was higher under President Carter, a Democrat, than is was under President Ford, a Republican. In fact the misery index peaked under President Carter at 20.76 and has been lower every since. The Democrats had shot themselves in the foot.

Today the misery index is 8.92 and at the level of the Bush years. Although this is a valid index it doesn't take into account the other aspects of society. For example, high school dropout rate, crime and illegal drug use would show a different picture of America than the DOW shows. Simply using the number of psychiatrists per thousand people would be a useful measure or the number of suicides per thousand people, especially suicide among young people. These indices measure more than economic prosperity. What good is a prosperous economic society if people are not happy living in it?

We could look at Valium use. We could look at the sales of anti-depression drugs. All these numbers are available but do not get the air time that football scores get. This is because broadcasters like happy news. No broadcaster wants to announce the daily suicide rate. Suicide is indeed something that we hear very little about.

So while the DOW is up is everything OK. Yes. How do we know that? Because the DOW is up. People are working and everybody is making money. The rich are getting richer a sure sign that things are fine. If people can't be happy in this environment then they have a problem, not society.

We have just suffered what is being called the greatest economic collapse since the great depression. What happened?

Well a lot of investing became based on the housing market. The theory is simple. Housing prices have always gone up. So if you buy a financial instruments like CDOs (collateralized debt obligations) or MBSs (mortgage backed securities) they would go up with housing prices. These were collateralized by a house whose value is increasing. How could you lose? If the buyer defaults, the bank forecloses, sells the house and you get your money back. What could possible go wrong here?

It is true that housing prices historically increase.

Then politics entered the equation. The Left felt that many poor people could not buy a house and the reason was that they did not qualify under the current lending standards. For example, you have to have a certain income, have been in the same job for two years and be able to put down 20% of the house's value as a down payment. Most poor people cannot do that.

So the Democrats, who have a lot of influence with Fannie Mae and Freddie Mac put pressure on them to lower their standards. This is very important and you don't often hear a lot about that.

Fannie Mae and Freddie Mac are quasi government agencies. They buy mortgages from the lending institutions. When the lending institutions have lent all their money out what do they do? Quit making more loans? No they sell their mortgages to Fannie Mae and Freddie Mac. They then use this money to make more mortgages. But Fannie and Freddie, as they are called, will not buy the mortgage unless the lender meets their standards.

When Fannie and Freddie lowered their standards, under political pressure from the Democrats, that allowed lending institutions to lower their standards for lending. The thinking became "if Fannie and Freddie will buy this paper, then we will write this loan.

This got completely out of control. Soon lending institutions were running ads that said "no down payment, no credit check, no income verification." After all what did they care Freddie and Fannie were going to buy this paper and the associated risk.

Our system of checks and balances failed us. Everybody was making money. Even President Bush was calling America "the ownership society" as more and more poor people bought houses. Meanwhile, Fannie and Freddie were bundling these mortgages and selling them to Wall Street to get their money back. So you could actually invest on bundles of home mortgages. Not only that, these bundles could be used as backing for bonds. The good times had finally arrived. Everybody was happy and nobody wanted to question what was going on.

What was going on was people who were not qualified were getting home loans. Since it was expected that home values always rose, how could you lose? People begin buying a second house just for investment. Holding it for a couple of years and selling it at a profit. The housing bubble began which pushed up the value of homes as demand for homes increased. Nobody wanted to stop or even slow down this economic miracle that was bringing prosperity to everyone, especially everyone on Wall Street.

Adding to this lunacy was something called "credit default swaps". The idea here is that a form of insurance was created. You could buy a policy that guaranteed a loan. If you did not get paid back, then the insurance company would pay you the loan amount for a very small premium. In fact, you did not even have to be a party to the transaction. Anyone could buy a credit default swap an any loan.

A very smart man whose name I forget did a very simple thing. He graphed income increases against home prices. Soon the spread became obvious. Home prices were rising faster that incomes and the spread was increasing. He quickly realized that at some point people would not be able to buy a home because they would not be able to make the payments. To him this meant that home prices would have to fall but this entire process was formulated on the idea that home prices would continue to rise.

He actually went to Wall Street who were buying these loans from Fannie and Freddie and later directly from the lending institutions themselves, bypassing Fannie and Freddie, and showed them what he had discovered. They listened and told him that he was wrong. This was more wishful thinking than objective reasoning on the part of Wall Street. If they thought that he was right, then they should immediately stop what they were doing and yet they were making a fortune. Furthermore, everybody was being paid on commission so the more of this you did, the more money you would make.

All it would take at this point was for home values to fall and the entire house of cards would come tumbling down. And who would lose? Among others, the insurance companies who wrote the credit default swaps since they would have to pay up.

So the man left Wall Street and went back home. So sure was he that he was right, he bought all the credit default swaps he could get his hands on. When it finally crashed, he made billions, paying a small amount in premiums for the credit default swaps, and making the full amount of the loan when it failed. It was beautiful.

One company writing credit defaults was AIG. They lost billions and had to be bailed out by the federal government.

So what caused the crash? Well first these people, like the poor who should have never gotten the loan in the first place, began to default on their mortgages. Housing prices began to fall as these houses were put on the market by the lending institutions. As it snowballed, those who bought homes as an investment found that the home value was less than they owed on the home so they would never be able to sell the investment home at a profit. So they walked away and defaulted as well. This increased the snowball effect.

Soon panic set it. The bubble had burst. All the financial instruments on Wall Street began losing value. This loss had to be shown on their books which caused the stock price of their companies to drop. This caused people to sell that stock which caused the stock price to fall even more.

The panic had hit. Soon major banks on Wall Street were talking about bankruptcy as well as AIG who had insured this paper with credit default swaps. It could no longer be ignored, the American economy was headed for a crash. It was a mathematical certainty.

The government was forced to step in and bail everyone out at the cost of trillions from the taxpayer. These companies were all called "too big to fail". It should be noted that that is not a term from capitalism, that is a political term. Under capitalism they would have been allowed to fail and medium sized banks, who had made good business decisions and were in good shape, would have moved in and taken over those markets and gotten bigger.

But politics ruled the day. Letting them fail would have brought on an even more severe situation and an angry public would have gotten its revenge by kicking all those politicians out of office. That is why the term "too big to fail" is a political term and not a term from the theory of capitalism or business.

So is the problem solved? Well the same people who brought us this mess are still there. The stock market is up simply because billions of tax payer dollars have been pumped into it. Some people have said that this is like giving a blood transfusion to someone who is bleeding internally. It's like a tire that has a small leak and goes flat. Pumping in more air will work in the short term but the tire is going to go flat again. .What you have to do is fix the hole.

Well we have not fixed the hole.

That would require massive financial regulation of these institutions and they are already gearing up to fight such a change, claiming that this is government intervention in the free market.

25

The Minimum Wage

"If a minimum wage worked, why don't we just set it a $10,000 a month and we would all be rich" - Bill Pirkle

What a great campaign slogan – vote for me and I will force a person to pay you more money. Thus is born the minimum wage. In our state of Washington it's $7.25 an hour.

The minimum wage is the reason that young people, particularly young Blacks, are unemployed. Thus, these young hang out and often get into trouble. Why is this the reason? Because these people are not worth $7.25 an hour. They often have no skills that are needed and thus do menial work. It's an averaging process - 90% of the menial workers make more money and all it costs is that 5% of the people are permanently unemployed. Except in the case of the young where it's more like 60% make more while 40% are unemployed. You have to keep the voting majority employed and well paid.

The minimum wage was enacted in America in 1938. Justified on social health and not economics, most countries now have a minimum wage. It has caught on and spread like wildfire. Why wouldn't it? These are no doubt democracies and they have more poor people than rich people.

It has several disadvantages. First, it causes unemployment, especially among the poor, since many small businesses can't afford that salary given what they are getting from the employee in skills. If there was no minimum wage, everybody would have a job. What would they make? Well that depends on what they can do and how many people can do that also. This is how the marketplace works. And remember they all had a chance at a free 12 year education. Some might make $1.00 an hour.

The employer puts up a sign "Help Wanted, $1.00 an hour." If nobody applied for the job, the employer would be forced to make it $2.00 an hour. Then $3.00 and perhaps $4.00 until someone took the job. The marketplace would set the salary. If everybody had good skills that were needed, the salaries would go up. If the workplace is full of unemployed high school dropouts, then these dropouts would make very little. The message would be, stay in school and get a skill.

What this would do is get everybody into the workplace. There they can learn some skills that would make them worth more money later in their careers. A kid could hang around a garage cleaning and sweeping and learn to be a mechanic. Another kid might hang around a restaurant cutting up vegetables and learn to be a cook. Currently, they are hanging around the shopping center and learning nothing. This guarantees a lower class for the Democrats to help, for their votes, of course.

Historically, mankind has used the apprentice approach. A young kid offers himself up as an apprentice to someone who has a skill, called the master. This approach worked for centuries. The master gets someone to help do the rote work and the apprentice learns to be a master while making some money. It's perfect.

Then come the Liberals. They claim that the apprentice is actually an employee so the master has to pay them the minimum wage and pay their workman's compensation, social security taxes, etc. Next the master needs an accountant. When the smokes settles it's too expensive for the master to deal with.

The liberal substitute the trade school approach. Here the kid goes to trade school to learn to be a master. Trade schools cost money. So now the kid is paying money instead of making money. This creates the trade school industry and creates jobs, the now chief role of government. Kids who can't afford trade school remains poor. If the kids go into the military, their veteran's benefits will pay for trade school. This is one way to raise an army.

There was a time when high schools had shops classes and some still do. But many schools have dropped this given that there are trade schools. No doubt the trade school association lobbied for this change to eliminate the competition from high schools.

Asians have an interesting way around this. Their kids work in the family business and for free. If mom and dad own a Chinese restaurant, their kids often work at the restaurant but not as employees. This is perfectly legal. What is not legal is to have that arrangement using someone else's kids.

Politicians get votes by mandating a minimum wage which create unemployed poor people that have to be serviced by the nanny state, getting them even more votes. What a great system.

Chapter 26

The Line Item Veto

"Tonight I ask you to give me what forty-three governors have: Give me a line-item veto this year. Give me the authority to veto waste, and I'll take the responsibility, I'll make the cuts, I'll take the heat."

What is the line item veto? In spending bills passed by Congress items are listed showing what this money will be spent for and how much money will be spent. This is especially true in budget bills, say, the appropriation bill for the Defense Department.

At the present time the President must sign the entire bill as one thing or veto it. Often there are spending items, cleverly placed in a bill that must pass, say, a bill to raise the ceiling on the national debt. This bill cannot be vetoed in a practical sense. There are many bills, like war funding bills, that are politically impossible to veto. So the pork spending, slipped in by a clever arrangement somewhere, passes also.

Several Presidents have claimed that what they need to control spending is a line item veto which would allow them to veto a particular spending item without vetoing the entire bill.

Congress fights any efforts to have this saying that it would be a transfer of power from the legislative to the executive branch. It would, to be sure, have a tremendous impact on Congressional politics. The whole place is one giant deal. One gets support for a bill by placing something in there for everybody. This is nearly always money that would go back to the states in the form of pork. To vote against it would be killing money that would go back to the local voters. Political suicide.

Notice that the rightness or wrongness of the legislation takes a back seat to everything else, like pork spending. Any legislator who objects to a bill can be made to vote for it by putting in some pork money for their state. If the President could veto a particular line item, the President could remove this spending. But then what would be the basis of politicking in Congress. You are a powerful member of Congress or the Senate if you can get this stuff in the bill in the first place. If the President is just going to remove it, then you effectively lose your power. In Washington, it's all about power.

Thus the Congress is reluctant to allow the line item veto. It is interesting that some Presidents do not even want it. These "profiles in courage" do not want to take the heat for vetoing a line item. Now they can say that the Congress put this in and I had no choice but to sign it into law. With the line item veto, this spending would be the President's fault since he had the power to remove it. The President, not the Congress, would be responsible for annual deficits and the growth in the national debt. Many Presidents do not want the line item veto and Congress certainly does not want it. So the deficits continue and the national debt continues to rise.

All but 7 states have the line item veto for their governors.

In 1996 the line item veto was passed by Congress. President Clinton used it to strike 82 items from the budget. But it was struck down by the Supreme Court by a 6 to 3 vote as being unconstitutional. President George W. Bush made the statement that he would not enforce parts of a bill that he did not agree with which would have been a form of a line item veto. But the President's role is to enforce the laws. If he signed the bill then it is the law. So it would be unconstitutional for a President to pick and choose which laws he will enforce.

There have been efforts to revive the line item veto but all have failed. It is more like an effort to make it look to the public that Congress is trying to control spending than it is an effort to actually control spending. What would be cut from any bill is pork spending. It is this pork spending that keeps the incumbent in office. It is his or her power to get federal monies into their state that makes them valuable to the people. In these days of runaway pork spending, few are sincerely trying to get a line item veto in place though all may say they are.

Some say that rather than Congress using this pork to keep themselves in office, that the President himself would use this to raise money for himself and his party. That is to say, that if you contribute some money to my campaign or my party, I will keep this item in the bill otherwise it's gone. Thus, the abuse would merely shift from the Congress to the Executive branch. This means that the money raised would not be enjoyed by Congress but enjoyed by the President. This is the real transfer of power that is at issue - money.

On June 25, 1998, the United States Supreme Court in Clinton, et al. v. City of New York, et al., held that the Line Item Veto Act, violated the Presentment Clause of the Constitution. The Clause requires that every bill which has passed the House and Senate before becoming law must be presented to the President for approval or veto, but is silent on whether the President may amend or repeal provisions of bills that have passed the House and Senate in identical form. The Court interpreted silence on this issue as equivalent to an express prohibition.

There is an argument put forth by some members of Congress to justify pork spending. They argue that with out pork barrel spending only the President could spend money.

Currently projects, now typically funded by pork barrel spending would be put into the budget submitted by the president. That will mean that the project filtered up through some bureaucracy having gone through many reviews and approvals to survive and become part of the budget. This process gives the executive branch a lot of power since the President can keep it alive, especially for a campaign contribution.

So, asks the Congress, why can't we put a project in the budget ourselves and we can get the campaign contribution. So they add projects to a bill that are earmarked for a particular district, or city or county or state. Then when the congressman runs for re-election he or she gets to claim credit for that.

At this point that may seem fair. But there is a bigger problem here. It is well known that it is very difficult to replace an incumbent. First, they have name recognition. Then they have the support of their party (in most cases) and can get money from the party. Then they can claim experience over the challenger. And finally they can claim credit for many projects in the district or state. All this makes it difficult for a nobody to challenge them.

This creates a fundamental weakness in our democracy. The Congress is supposed to represent the people. As the beliefs and attitudes of the public change because of life experiences, then the government should reflect those changes. This is done by electing new politicians. But as it becomes very difficult to do, then the government does not reflect the beliefs and attitudes of the public. Hence, the government, specifically the Congress does not represent the people. This is bad.

This has caused some to call for term limits for congress. Others then say that there are already term limits because they run for office and can be replaced by the voters. This is a cruel joke for the reasons that I have just explained.

Chapter 27

The National Debt

"Let's all be happy and live within our means, even if we have to borrow the money to do it with." - Artemus Ward

We hear a lot of talk about the national debt and we should understand what it is exactly. The first thing to do is to distinguish between the annual deficit and the national debt. The government takes in money through taxes and it spends monies based on bills passed by the Congress and signed into law by the President. What if, for any given year, the spending bills are greater that the tax income for that year? When that happens a deficit occurs. When a deficit occurs the government has to borrow the money to make up the difference.

Although this is complicated, the government borrows money by selling bonds and treasury notes. People buy these bonds and we refer to this as their buying our debt. Both Americans, people all over the world and even nations buy our debt. It is considered a safe place to invest money since the U.S. Government is not going to go bankrupt. This debt, called the national debt, is the accumulation of all the annual deficits that the government occurred by spending more money in any given year than it took in in taxes.

Today this national debt is about 13 trillion dollars. Divide that number by the approximately 300 million people in America and each person's share is about $41,000 per person. In other words, it would take every man, woman and child in

America to come up with $41,000 each to pay off the national debt. It is a lot of money.

But how much is a trillion dollars? Senator Everett Dirksen, U.S. Senator from Illinois, once said "a billion here and a billion there and pretty soon you are talking about real money." He was referring to the way the rich American Empire spent money as if it grew on trees.

Well we seem to have cranked that up a notch, or better put, an order of magnitude. We now talk about a trillion here and an trillion there, especially when talking about rescue packages and stimulus packages. It makes one wonder just how much is a trillion dollars?

We often hear that if you stack a million dollars end to end it would reach to the moon several times. But who has a grasp on how far it is to the moon? We often measure things in what is becoming a standard unit of measurement, along with the centimeter, the inch, the foot, the mile and the kilometer, the football field. We often hear about how many football fields it would take to do this or that.

Still we do not get a grasp on how much money a trillion dollars is. Someone once described it like this. Suppose you spent a million dollars a day. This turns out to be a daunting task. On the first day you buy a $800,000 house and a $200,000 car. That's a million dollars. So tomorrow you buy a yacht and an airplane. Fine. But what's next? Well on the third day you could buy diamonds and gold bars. Fine, but there is still tomorrow. What next? It turns out to be a full time job spending a million dollars a day.

But let's assume that this could be done and let's assume that you have been doing this since the birth of Christ. Throughout the Roman Empire, throughout the Middle Ages, throughout the Renaissance, throughout the American

Revolution, the Civil War, WWI, the Great Depression, WWII, the 50's, 60's, 70's, 80's, 90's and to date. A million dollars a day you spent through all this time. You still would not have spent a trillion dollars.

Do the math. Multiply 2010 times 365 times 1,000,000. You would have spent, spending a million dollars a day since the birth of Christ, about 734 billion dollars, a few billion short of a trillion. (a trillion is 1000 billion.)

This is far short of the stimulus package being recommended by Congress, lately 790 billion.

This may give you a handle on what we spent to jump start the economy. Given all the other spending that has occurred to solve our economic problems, bailing out Fannie and Freddie, the 700 billion for the banks began under Bush and continuing under Obama, we are reaching the point where the government could have just bought all the outstanding mortgages and let the people live there without foreclosures, which is what started this mess in the first place.

Why didn't we just do that? Because the size of this problem has been underestimated by the experts from the very beginning. First, they said that the 700 billion to the banks would fix this. Then they said, no, it would take more to jump start the economy. It's amazing that these experts cannot even get a handle of the size of the problem they are trying to solve.

And what if this doesn't work? No problem, just throw another trillion dollars at it. But let's not forget the words of Senator Dirksen, paraphrased it reads "a trillion here and a trillion there and pretty soon you are talking about real money."

But we have plenty of trees to make paper and many high speed printing presses to print paper money. President Nixon removed America from the gold standard so there is no limit to the amount of money we can print, as long a Communist China will continue to buy our debt.

It's a curious quirk of history that the capitalist West is now living off the savings of the Communist East. Perhaps Karl Mark is laughing in his grave.

So how did the national debt ever get that big? Well, the Congress seems to have no will power to not spend money. Some of this money is needed to run the departments of government. Other monies are spent on what are called pork spending projects. Pork refers to monies spent by the government that benefits projects back home in a particular congressperson's or Senator's district or state. This money can be used at election time for the incumbents to claim that this is why you should return me to Congress. I have bought all this money to pay for all these projects into our state. These projects range from the reasonably justifiable to the absurd.

This gives rise to the professional politician who claims that previous experience in politics is a requirement for getting elected. These people know the system and how to work it to get more federal money back into the state.

For the money used to run the government, it either goes to pay salaries of government employees or is spent through contracts with the private sector to buy things that the government needs, like paper clips and F-18 jet fighters. This spending is income to private companies which they use to buy materials for production and to pay salaries of their employees. This spending creates jobs and in a time when creating jobs has become the chief function of government, it is difficult to cut.

All government spending has the ultimate effect of keeping the incumbent politicians in office. This is one of the many advantages the incumbent has over the challenger in an election. Another advantage is name recognition.

Some people think that the national debt is not a problem, saying that it is money that we owe ourselves. This is not true for several reasons. First, we owe this money to people all around the world, not just to ourselves. This is a real debt that has to be paid as these bonds mature. It becomes circular financing. As, say, 500 billion dollars in bonds mature which were issued years back, then we have to sell 500 billion dollars in bonds today to pay off those bonds. Parts of the debt are constantly coming due depending on whether these are 5 year bonds, 10 year bonds or 30 year bonds. Our national debt is constantly being refinanced. Since we cannot default on these bonds, this is priority spending. Other priority spending includes Social Security and Medicare. The interest on the debt today is 1.9 trillion dollars a year. The debt today is 13 trillion dollars. Of that 3.9 trillion dollars is held by foreign countries. The deficit today is 1.4 trillion dollars this year. That's another 1.4 trillion dollars added to the 13 trillion dollars in national debt.

As the famous senator Everett Dirksen once said. "A billion, a billion there, and pretty soon you are talking real money." Today's Congress has a tendency to think of a billion dollars as chump change.

There is a myth that there is a social security trust fund. Well, there is on paper in the form of IOUs. The government has, over the years, borrowed all that real money to continue the spending spree. The agreement is that in any year, the social security administration has first dibs on any tax revenues to meet their obligations for that year.

What is left after these mandatory obligations is what the government can spend to run the government. If there is not enough for that year, another deficit is occurred and that money is added to the national debt, increasing it. That money is raised by selling more government securities to the world which holds our debt. So the debt is not money that we owe ourselves.

The other problem with the national debt is what is called servicing the debt. Like all debt interest has to be paid. So the question is what is the annual interest on the national debt? Although is varies with interest rates and other factors it is about 1.9 trillion dollars a year today. This means that of the taxes paid by citizens this year, 1.9 trillion dollars is taken off the top to pay interest on the national debt. The federal spending this year is 3.5 trillion dollars. So the math says that 1.9/3.5 is 54%. So 54% of all the money collected in taxes this year will simply go to paying interest on the national debt. This too is priority spending and must be spent first. Then Social Security and Medicare, then other government programs.

There is no chance that America will ever pay off the national debt. As it gets larger, the amount of money each year to pay the interest on it increases. It is possible that 80 percent of the government's annual budget will be needed someday just to pay the interest. This money then is not available for spending on government programs that the public expects. Of course, when the annual percentage of the government budget reaches 100%, the government will have to shut down completely. Then tax dollars will go to nothing but paying that year's interest on the national debt.

Accounting tricks can be and are used. Curiously, as the annual budget increases, the interest share per year decreases. All we have to do is have a government budget of 6 trillion dollar budget next year, and the percentage that interest is of it is only 32% down from 54%. But to get that 6 trillion dollar budget, more bonds will have to be sold and in later years as those chickens come home to roost or just cheapen the currency and hunker down for inflation. We are just buying time. We are on a collision course with ourselves.

From time to time and very rarely, the government runs a surplus and can use a few billion dollars to pay down the debt. But most politicians would rather spend that money on pork barrel projects than to make that slight dent in the national debt.

The debt is often referred to as "the national credit card" and it is in a way. To please the public and thus stay in office, politicians can't say no. They spend more than they have in taxes. The difference becomes the annual deficit and is added each year to the national debt. The government sells bonds to finance the debt and the annual interest we pay goes up.

How long can this continue? It can continue as long as there are people in the world who will buy our government debt. They are a safe investment assuming you believe that the American government is not going to go bankrupt. They don't pay as much return on investments as other higher risk investment might pay but they are safer. In the days of everyone having a balanced portfolio, one should have a certain percentage of their investments in government securities.

But what happens if there becomes a better place to invest your money besides American government securities? What if it becomes better to invest in Chinese securities after the Communist topple there. Then we may run out of people who will buy our debt and the house of cards will come tumbling down. Remember our debt is currently being refinanced each year requiring us to sell more securities to retire securities previously sold. The amount of money needed for this varies. If, say, 10 years ago we ran a big deficit and sold a lot of bonds, then today there will be the requirement to sell an lot of bonds to retire that debt, or better said, to refinance that debt.

If at that time people around the world have lost faith in America and have a better place to invest their money, then we will default. One default will bring down the house of cards. So it's in our interest to keep the rest of the world weak so there is no other place for people to invest their money.

So we simply need a way to coerce people to buy our bonds. During WWII we had bond drives and appealed to people's patriotism to buy war bonds to finance the war.

Perhaps we can have terror bonds to finance the war on terror. Perhaps we can pass another law requiring pension funds to invest a certain percentage of their assets in government bonds. Perhaps we can pass a law requiring people to buy government bonds whether they want them or not. This is not actually a tax increase since you will get the money back when the bond matures. This is more like forced savings to keep the government afloat.

In the past when we were fighting communism, we could claim that we, and our military, are protecting you from communism. So you must help buy buying our debt. .But communism is gone. But, atlas, we have the war on terror. So now we can claim that we are leading the charge to fight terror, from which you benefit, so you should help us by buying our debt. We seem to always need and have a global enemy from which to save the world like a knight riding a white horse. Yea America.

Chapter 28

Illegal Immigration

"Give me your tired, your poor, your huddled masses yearning to breathe free - Emma Lazarus

This is a line from a poem inscribed on the statue of liberty. We are a nation of immigrants or at least descendants of immigrants. Everybody entered the country legally and blended in. Their first job was to learn English. Ellis Island was their getting off point and they were checked for dieses particularly tuberculosis. Those who were very sick were sent back. Much sadness occurred when everybody in a family got in except one who was sent back. What a lonely boat ride that must have been. Many jumped into the ocean and committed suicide.

This system worked for years but as the federal government grew to its current level of incompetence, the Immigration & Nationalization Service begin failing along with all the other government departments and agencies. Remember, as I said, that a dead animal rots all over at the same time.

Now we are stuck with a massive illegal immigrant problem. How did this happen? Well it just grew from a few Mexicans crossing the border illegally to more, then more. The problem grew so slowly that nobody noticed it.

So why can't we fix this. Well first they work hard and do jobs that Americans won't do. At least that is the story. The fact is that Mexican labor does jobs that many Americans will do. But Americans have been spoiled and there are many jobs they won't do despite the fact that we are in a recession. Since the Congress continues to extend unemployment benefits, many can survive on that.

But there are other reasons that we are not insisting that people do work that they may see as beneath them. We could just stop the unemployment payments. But, for example, what kind of image would be projected with Blacks working in the fields. It would look like the old South where slaves worked in the fields. That would lessen the perceived notion that the Civil Rights movement was successful. That would increase the perception that there is racism in America. With Mexicans we can argue that, first, they are not black and second, they are not even citizens.

These Mexicans make a real contribution to America's economy as President Bush was quick to point out when he failed to do anything about illegal immigration. Often a situation develops where it is not in the interest of either side of our checks and balances to solve a problem. The Republican businessmen need the cheap labor and the Democrats know that these people will support them since they will be dependent on government assistance. But they don't vote you say. Well, we are not sure how many illegal immigrants vote but their brothers and sisters in the Hispanic community do vote. Nobody wants to be seen as anti-Hispanic by supporting the idea of a fence at the border or military on the border. Indeed much compassion is shown for illegal immigrants. Their children can attend school, they can get treated in emergency rooms and there is other public assistance available to them.

To be sure these are nice people who work hard, who have strong family values, who are Christian and who are just trying to better their lot in life. But so are the millions left in Mexico. Should we have an open border policy and just let them all come over. And what about all those people who are trying to enter America legally and find themselves on long waiting lists?

There is so little real support to solving this problem that we can't even seem to identify them and make them carry an id card indicating their status. This is always met with the objection that such government behavior would lead to a national id card. Yet permanent residents carry a green card and that did not lead to a national ID card. Indeed, simply identifying illegal immigrants as a problem seems anti-Hispanic to many Americans.

Add to this the sanctuary cities. Here certain cities, often major cities, have announced that they will not even attempt to identify illegals and enforce federal immigration law. Of course many illegals take refuge in those cities where they feel safe.

So how are we going to fix this mess? We can't identify them for fear of being accused of profiling. We can't deny them benefits for fear of appearing inhuman. We can't stop the infiltration because we can't run the risk of hurting them at the border. They have to be handled with kid gloves. The most we can do is send them back but they will just try again hoping to have better luck getting through the next time.

There are 111 million Mexicans Mexico and everyone of them have a cousin who lives in America. That was a bit sarcastic but not far from the truth. And with the current increase in Mexican population in America, both legal and illegal, it will be true someday. The strategy will be get across the border and find your cousin.

Epilogue

Thomas Jefferson said it in the Declaration of Independence – "all experience has shown that men are more disposed to suffer, while evils are sufferable, than to right themselves by abolishing the forms to which they are accustomed."

This disposition keeps both men and women in abusive relationships that are harmful to their mental health and in some cases to their physical health as well. This disposition keeps people working at jobs that they hate and working for a boss that they hate as well. People are often afraid of change.

There have been several attempts to start 3rd parties in America but in the end they were unsuccessful because of this disposition, leaving us with the incompetent, corrupt Republicans and the incompetent, corrupt Democrats. We seem not to be able to abolish the forms to which we are accustomed.

But Jefferson says "while evils are sufferable". Apparently kids being kidnapped, raped and murdered, unsafe streets, failing schools and a national debt that is impossible to pay off are not evils enough. Apparently it will take more. Perhaps riots in the streets, marshal law, and curfews will do it after 2 or 3 years of that.

It will probably unfold like this. First, an economic collapse. This is possible since the same people who brought us this mess are still in power on Wall Street. Little has changed. The dollar will lose value because of how many they are printing to prop the economy up. Then there will be massive inflation for the same reason.

Next there will be layoffs and as prices go up due to inflation, there would be people without gasoline and enough food. This will cause riots in the streets. This has happened many times before all over the world. Take the French Revolution as an example.

To quell the riots, the governments will declare marshal law and curfews would be enacted. So we will have a little peace. But the question is how long will the marshal law last? A few days would be alright but what if it went on for say a year. Suddenly the government looks like an oppressive dictatorship and not a democracy.

What if a case could be made that America right now is too unstable to hold elections? So we cancel elections until things settle down. Then citizens will see America in an entirely new way. A dictatorship with no elections.

You may think that I am exaggerating mentioning canceling elections. So go to Google and search "canceling elections". !5,800,000 websites are found.

Then the guns will come out and the revolution begins. This is when we will be glad that there is a 2nd amendment. Knowing this the government may even try to pass emergency laws that say, of course you can keep your gun but you cannot take it outside your house on the street. Do that and you will be arrested and taken to the stadiums which as I have explained earlier, will be the mass detention centers.

Of course concealed carry permits will be cancelled So if you have to go out, you will have to take your chances.

The national leaders know this. They know that if 95% of the people have job and there are cheap imports to buy, everybody is happy, thus the evils are sufferable. Their job is easy, just keep this going. There is a national credit card to pump money into the economy to keep it running. They control the economy through the tax code and other regulations. They can keep this going as long as there are people around the world who will buy our debt. Right now America is the best place to invest your money. But this will not always be the case. Nations rise and fall. China who is just now waking up after centuries of sleep was once a great empire. Then Europe rose and dominated it. Now the West seems to be on the decline while the East is on the rise. If China, or perhaps we should say when China, sheds its communist government and becomes a democracy, then watch out. Their strength is in their culture. They respect their parents, obey authority, and work hard. Everything we don't do. Add to that that they are very smart. They have all the ingredients for greatness, piggy backing on all the technology developed by the West. Soon China's economy may be a better place to invest money than in America's economy. When that happens there will be no one to buy America's government debt. Without the influx of money to our government to keep the economy going strong, a giant adjustment will take place. This will involve a lot of suffering and wisdom will return to America.

This because a total change in government in terms of who now holds office will involve high unemployment for a while at least. These dissatisfied citizens will vote for a change in terms of whose running things. The developing wisdom will cause the voters to vote, not based on charisma or handsomeness, but on what the candidate says. Things said, unlike today, will have to make sense to the common man. This politico-cultural revolution will set America back on course but it could take decades or even centuries. This will be because the powerful East will now be dominating us. With their foot on our throat, getting back up will be hard to do.

These are the grand cycles that nations go through as history unfolds. Since the cycles are longer than the human life span, nobody has ever lives through an entire cycle. Some are fortunate to live through the upside and peak of a cycle like

Americans in the last 60 years. Some are unfortunate and live through the downside and bottom of the cycle, like the Chinese in the last 300 years. Only by studying history do the cycles reveal themselves.

At the peak of the cycle, people tend to think that these good times will go on forever. They drop their guard and get careless. They don't participate in elections. They don't keep up with current affairs. We see this today in America. Most citizens can name more quarterbacks in the national football leagues than they can name important members of Congress. Most Americans know more about the win/loss statistics of football and baseball teams than they know about statistics on the American economy.

Kids are not learning much at school but are having fun. It seems to be all about fun these days. You can use the available balance on your unsolicited credit care and buy happiness. When over-extended, refinance your house, pay off your credit cards and start over. But you can only play that card one time since the annual appreciation of your house may be less than your annual credit card spending rate.

It is often said that everyone wants to come to America. Well, that is no great surprise. What a fun place to live. Everyone would like to live in America in the same way that everyone would like to go to a great party. This is because we are at the peak of our economic cycle. Few will want to live here when we are on the downside. If fact, we can predict a mass exodus of people. This will hasten the decline since those leaving will be those with money, removing what will be much needed capital from the markets. Professionals will also leave. Doctors are always in demand around the world as are scientists. The professionals we will be left with, unfortunately, will be the lawyers. This is because while the human body and scientific principals are the same the world over, the law is drastically different the world over. An American lawyer can't just pick up and go practice the law in, say, China or England for that matter.

This will be good only in the sense that they will be many lawsuits going on in the downside of the economic cycle.

So when you hear that America's best days are still ahead, think who is telling you this. It will be a politician running for office, probably for re-election. Those in power have to say how great things are while those out of power talk about how bad things are and the solution is to put them in power. Yet little changes whether the Republicans or Democrats are in power. Yet third parties do not do well. But there will come a time when the voters will reject both current parties and look for a real change in leadership.

In this book I have tried to show the changes that have taken place since our victory in WWII. I have tried to look at many areas like schools, courts and the workplace to name a few. I have tried to paint a picture of reality for people who may not understand these things and how they relate. A book that covers such a vast variety of subjects cannot go into a great level of detail on any one topic but not to worry. We have Google. Any topic in this book can be researched there for those who want to learn more. Hopefully, this book will stimulate a desire to know more. Hopefully, this book will excite people's curiosity about the reality they live in. These cycles, however are not stoppable. We can't stop history from unfolding. But this is about surviving. Surviving is a matter of being able to predict what will happen next and positioning yourself accordingly. It is said that only the paranoid survive. That may or may not be true, but many will think me paranoid by what I have said in this book. Others will agree because they have seen and are seeing these things going on right now.

The problem is those people who are afraid of change. As Thomas Jefferson said – "all experience has shown that men are more disposed to suffer, while evils are sufferable, than to right themselves by abolishing the forms to which they are accustomed."

But it is human nature to adjust to evil. Things have to get very bad indeed before these evils are no longer sufferable. It's like the frog in the pan of water. As you slowly increase the heat, the frog gets use to it. We too get used to schools failing, increases in crime rate, insecurity in our job in the workplace. If it happens slowly enough it can get very bad. In theory we can sink to the level of a third world country. Remember the point I made earlier that problems become normal to people who can't remember a time when the problems did not exist. At each rung on the latter on the downside, there will be many people to whom this state of affairs is normal. If these people make up more than 50% of the voters then we are in big trouble because they will not see the need for a change.

Historically, nations on the downside of the economic cycle are ripe for invasion from a neighboring country. We do have a neighboring country eligible for this and that is Mexico. I am ruling out an invasion from Canada. But Mexico is a theoretical possibility. Then they can get the Southern United States back which we took from them.

So history is unfolding before us and we must recall the adage – those who forget history are doomed to repeat it.

But there are those who have faith in Democracy. The system is dynamic they say, it adjusts to changes. This is true. Here is a good example of how the system will adjust. The high school dropout rate in California is about 50%.These kids do not have a high school diploma. They can get a GED if they are motivated but if they were motivated they would have stayed in school. Many businesses require a high school diploma for employment. But you do not need a high school diploma to flip burgers or stock shelves. These dropouts vote and as those numbers increase, they will become a significant voting bloc for candidates to appeal to. Now all the ingredients are in place for an adjustment. A candidate, hungry for votes in these days of tight elections, proposes that it is discrimination to not hire someone who can do a job, simply because he/she does not have a high school diploma. He/she will further argue that it was the school system that failed the kids and not a failure on the part of the kids themselves. Indeed, many dropouts, it will be argued, come from broken homes and poor homes and this is not the dropout's fault. Why then should the dropout be punished for a failure of society? Therefore, we need a law that makes it illegal to require a high school diploma if the applicant can otherwise do the work required by the position. So now these kids can at least get a menial job.

What we always forget in situations such as this are what are called unintended consequences. This law might make sense but it will motivate others to drop out. Why? Well they no longer need a high school diploma to get a job. The dropout rate can be expected to increase. Many do not like school anyway. In my day, high school dropouts were rare because of the stigma attached. But that stigma is gone. We are well on the way to having a situation where dropping out of high school is normal and maybe even cool. Only those who want to go on to college need stay in and finish.

Much of what I have written in this book was caused by unintended consequences. For example welfare laws were written so that the government would not give money to families where there was a man in the house. The idea was that the man should go out a get a job and support his family. Sounds like a plan. But fathers soon realized that the family would be better off if he left so that the mother could qualify for welfare. Next we have a great number of single moms trying to raise a family. So why do the kids do poorly in school? Well because many of them come from, you guessed it, single parent households. This then becomes an excuse for poor performance in school in many cases. When the poor kid turns to crime, the excuse will be used again to get a lenient sentence.

Several people who did me the favor of reading this book before publication were surprised that I do not offer solutions to all the problems that I have identified. I purposely avoided solutions for this simple reason. People may agree with the identification of a problem but not agree with the solution I would offer. Then they may have an unfavorable opinion of the book itself. I want people to read this book and not be turned off by it because they don't like my solutions.

Add to that that it is not my jobs to solve problems. That is the job of elected officials. My role here is to identify problems and show what are, in my opinion, the causes. I am only showing the reader some things to look at. You may disagree with both the problems and their causes. In the very beginning of the book I asked the reader to just look around and see for themselves.

We are entering the Age of Aquarius in 2013. We are leaving the Age of Pisces. Each age lasts for about 2000 years. For most of the Age of Pisces, the West dominated the East. Now the West is in decline while the East is on an assent. Many people think that great things happen at the beginning of a new age. Christ's birth coincides with the beginning of the Age of Pisces.

The Age of Aquarius may mark the beginning of a great change in East/West relations. In the end it is those who have the best belief system that wins. Wars are about the survival of belief systems.

Shakespeare said that our fate lies in ourselves and not in our stars. The way we are behaving, it may be better if our fate lay in our stars, but in this case, we may lose either way.

The End